The Church in Prayer

Carthusian Monks

Preface by Pope Francis

NOTES ON PRAYER
Volume 6

Our Sunday Visitor
Huntington, Indiana

Scripture quotations are from *The ESV® Bible (The Holy Bible, English
Standard Version®)*, copyright © 2001 by Crossway, a publishing
ministry of Good News Publishers. Used by permission. All rights
reserved.

Our Sunday Visitor Publishing Division
Our Sunday Visitor, Inc.
200 Noll Plaza
Huntington, IN 46750
1-800-348-2440

ISBN: 978-1-63966-278-4 (Inventory No. T2941)
eISBN: 978-1-63966-279-1
LCCN: 2024948807

Cover and interior design: Amanda Falk
Cover art: Adobestock

OSV extends thanks to the Catholc Truth Society for its collaboration
in producing this book.

Printed in the United States of America

Contents

Contents

Preface by Pope Francis

———

Prayer is the breath of faith, its most proper expression. It's like a silent cry that comes out from the heart of whoever trusts and believes in God. It's not easy to find words to express this mystery. How many definitions of prayer we can gather from the saints and masters of spirituality, as well as from the reflections of theologians! Nevertheless, it is always and only in the simplicity of those who live prayer that prayer finds expression. The Lord, moreover, warned us that, when we pray, we must not waste words, deluding ourselves that thus we will be heard. He taught us rather to prefer silence and to entrust ourselves to the Father, who knows the kind of things we need even before we ask for them (see Mt 6:7–8).

The Ordinary Jubilee of 2025 is already at the door. How to prepare ourselves for this event, so important for the life of the Church, if not by means of prayer? The year 2023 was set aside for a rediscovery of the conciliar teachings, contained especially in the four constitutions of the Second Vatican Council. It is a way of keeping alive the mandate that the Fathers gathered at the council wished to place in our hands, so that by means of its implementation, the Church might recover its youthful face and proclaim, in a language adapted to the men and women of our time, the beauty of the Faith.

Now is the time to prepare for a year that will be dedicated entirely to prayer. In our own time the need is being felt more and more strongly for a true spirituality capable of responding to the great questions which confront us every day of our lives, questions caused by a global scenario that is far from serene. The ecological-economic-social crisis aggravated by the recent pandemic; wars, especially the one in Ukraine, which sow death, destruction, and poverty; the culture of indifference and waste that tends to stifle aspirations for peace and solidarity and keeps God at the margins of personal and social life. ... These phenomena combine to bring about a ponderous atmosphere that holds many people back from living with joy and serenity. What we need, therefore, is that our prayer should rise up with greater insistence to the Father so that he will listen to the voice of those who turn to him, confident of being heard.

This year dedicated to prayer is in no way intended to affect the initiatives which every particular Church considers it must plan for in its own daily pastoral commitment. On the contrary, it aims to recall the foundation on which the various pastoral plans should be developed and find consistency. This is a time when, as individuals or communities, we can rediscover the joy of praying in a variety of forms and expressions. A time of consequence enabling us to increase the certainty of our faith and trust in the intercession of the Virgin Mary and the saints. In short, a year in which we can have the experience almost of a "school of prayer," without taking anything for granted (or at cut-rate), especially with regard to our way of praying, but making our own, every day, the words of the disciples when they asked Jesus: "Lord, teach us to pray" (Lk 11:1).

In this year we are invited to become more humble and to leave space for the prayer that flows from the Holy Spirit. It is he who knows how to put into our hearts and onto our lips the right words so that we will be heard by the Father. Prayer in the Holy Spirit is what unites us with Jesus and allows us to adhere to the will of the Father. The Spirit is the interior Teacher who indicates the way to follow. Thanks to him the prayer of even just one person can become the prayer of the entire Church, and vice versa. There is nothing like prayer according to the Spirit to make Christians feel united as the one family of God. It is God who knows how to recognize everyone's needs and how to make those needs become the invocation and intercession of all.

I am certain that bishops, priests, deacons, and catechists will find more effective ways this year of placing prayer as the basis of the announcement of hope which the 2025 Jubilee intends to make resonate in this troubled time. For this reason, the contribution of consecrated persons will be of great value, particularly communities of contemplative life. I hope that in all the shrines of the world, privileged places for prayer, initiatives should be increased so that every pilgrim can find an oasis of serenity and return with a heart filled with consolation. May prayer, both personal and communal, be unceasing, without interruption, according to the will of the Lord Jesus (see Lk 18:1), so that the kingdom of God may spread, and the Gospel reach every person seeking love and forgiveness.

As an aid for this Year of Prayer, some short texts have been produced which, with their simple language, will make possible entry into the various dimensions of prayer. I thank the authors for their contribution and willingly place into your hands these "notes" so that everyone can rediscover the beauty of trusting in the Lord with humility and joy. And don't forget to pray also for me.

Vatican City
September 27, 2023

Franciscus

The Mystery and Gift of Prayer

———

Christ Jesus, high priest of the new and eternal covenant, taking human nature, introduced into this earthly exile that hymn which is sung throughout all ages in the halls of heaven. He joins the entire community of mankind to himself, associating it with His own singing of this canticle of divine praise. For He continues His priestly work through the agency of His Church, which is ceaselessly engaged in praising the Lord and interceding for the salvation of the whole world. (*Sacrosanctum Concilium*, 83)

These words of the Second Vatican Council, which St. Paul VI cited in his promulgation of the revised Liturgy of the Hours, describe, in a wonderful synthesis, the gift and mystery of the prayer of the Church, and of every faithful Christian.

The mystery of prayer
Already this text of the council can give us a glimpse

that prayer is a mystery because it has its origin and its roots in the very Heart of God, in the "hymn which is sung throughout all ages in the halls of heaven," which resounds eternally in the very Mystery of God, and which he alone, the Triune God, knows. For this reason he alone can sing it and teach it to us.

It is in Christ's Paschal mystery that the Father has opened "the doors of eternity" to us and revealed the mystery of his intimate life, has revealed what is this "eternal song of praise." As far as our poverty is given to understand what has been revealed to us, there, in the "silence of the eternal ages" that surrounds the mystery of God (cf. Rom 16:25), one Word alone resounds, that of the Father who says to the Son, "You are my Son" (Ps 2:7). This is the sole Word that the Father eternally speaks, and uttering this Word "exhausts" all the Father's activity. The Father does not and cannot do anything other than "speak" his sole Word, his only-begotten Word: "The Father spoke one Word, which was His Son, and *speaks it always* in eternal silence," as St. John of the Cross stupendously puts it.

And the Son, in turn, responds to him with a single word: "Abba-Father."

The Spirit is the silence that allows the Father to utter the Word "You are my Son" (cf. St. Ignatius of Antioch, *Letter to the Christians of Magnesia*, VIII, 2) and allows the Son to listen to it and therefore to recognize himself as such, as Son of the Father, responding, "Father-Abba."

In turn, the Son is the silence in which the Father can "speak himself forth completely" (St. Cyril of Alexandria, *Commentary on 2nd Cor.,* PG 74, 923–924) and without reservation. The Verbum, the eternal Word, is the "Amen" (Rv 3:14), the perfect "Yes" (cf. 2 Cor 1:19), the welcome without limit of the Father's Word: "You are my Son." If he were to speak his own words, he could not fully welcome the word of the Father, he could not be *the* Word *of* the Father: "The word that you hear is not mine but the Father's who sent me" (Jn 14:24).

The Word has no Words of his own. He is only the Word *of* the Father because he can speak only what he has heard: "I declare to the world what I have heard from him. ... I do nothing on my own authority but speak just as the Father taught me ... the word that you hear is not mine but the Father's who sent me" (Jn 8:26, 28; 14:24).

The Son, the Word uttered, of his own possesses only pure silence, he is pure silence, because he stands before the Father like a silent echo that reflects in a perfectly pure way what the Father says to him: "You are my Son." He stands before the Father as a silent and serene mirror, most pure (cf. Wis 7:26), which perfectly reflects what the Father is, what the Father does. "Truly, truly, I say to you, the Son can do nothing of his own accord, but only what he sees the Father doing. For whatever the Father does, that the Son does likewise" (Jn 5:19). This dialogue between the Father and the Son in the Spirit, this eternal "self-speaking," constitutes the whole life of God, everything that exists "in the beginning."

"Abba-Father" is therefore "the song of praise that resounds eternally in the halls of heaven." It is "the hymn of thanksgiving that rises to the Father from his ever-living Christ" (Liturgy).

For this reason, "Abba, Father!" is the only and the true prayer that perfectly glorifies the Father. And the gift that Christ has given to his Church is the possibility of being able to sing it with him, through him and in him.

Already from these succinct reflections we can glimpse that the prayer that Christ has left as a legacy to his Church, which safeguards it incessantly, is his Mystery as Son, it is he himself. ... In giving us his Son, the Father has given us the very mystery of prayer, of the possibility of praying, that is, of entering into real communion with him, with the God whom no one has ever seen nor can see, but whom we can now, in Christ, moved by the Holy Spirit, in all truth call "Abba!"

Our prayer and that of the Church is therefore "union with the prayer of Christ insofar as it makes us participate in his mystery" (*Catechism of the Catholic Church*, 2718). But when we meditate on and discuss the prayer of the Church, we are talking about our own prayer, because the boundary between the Church and the individual Christian is permeable and transparent.

Talking about the mystery of the Church is equivalent to talking about the mystery of every Christian soul. In fact, "every soul, through the mystery of the sacramental bond, carries fully within itself the whole Church, which is one in all and entirely in individuals" (St. Peter Damian, *Dominus Vobiscum*, PL 145, 235).

The gift of prayer

Prayer is a gift because, with his Incarnation, Christ has given to his Church, and through the Church to every man, this "song of praise," "Abba-Father," which he eternally sings to his Father in the halls of heaven.

Christ "introduced [it] into this earthly exile" because his joy is living with men (cf. Prv 8:31). Our prayer therefore arises first of all from the longing that God feels for man, from the desire that Christ has to be with us. Not the desire to be adored, praised and served, but simply the desire to "be with us," to be able to sing with us, almost as if he had "need" of us, of our voice, so that his song to the Father may be complete and perfect.

Christ "introduced into this earthly exile that hymn which is sung throughout all ages in the halls of heaven" in order to offer us the possibility of renewing the dialogue with the true Father, with the Father whom he alone, Jesus, knows (cf. Mt 11:27). He knows him and knows that his joy is living with men (cf. Prv 8:31). This affirmation of uncreated Wisdom therefore contains the heart of the mystery of prayer. Prayer, in its deepest core, is nothing other than our welcoming of this desire of God to be with us, to be with each of us personally, to give us himself, to make us participants in his Life, in his Reality, in his "nature," as Saint Peter says (2 Pt 1:4). His joy is in being able to share life with us, to live our life so as to be able to give us his in exchange, to "drink our bitterness and give us the sweetness of His grace," as Saint Ambrose said (*Expositio in Psalmum 118*, PL 15, 1463). This desire of God to live with us is the source and wellspring of prayer.

"My House Shall Be Called a House of Prayer" (Is 56:7)

———

"But will God indeed dwell with man on the earth?" (2 Chronicles 6:18)

"What kind of house will you build for me, says the Lord, or what is the place of my rest?" (Acts 7:49; cf. Isaiah 66:1)

Yes, it is really true that God wants to live with men on earth, but only he can build the house in which he wants to live with us. In fact, "Unless the LORD builds the house, / those who build it labor in vain" (Ps 127:1).

The house of God is the Church of the living God, Saint Paul says (cf. 1 Tm 3:15). And God himself wanted this house of his to be a house of prayer (Is 56:7; Mk 11:17; Lk 19:46; Mt 21:13). Prayer, the dialogue between God and man, the union between God and man, is therefore the very essence of the Church, its reason for being, outside of which it would have no cause to exist. To speak of the prayer of the Church is therefore to peer into its very mystery, a mystery "in which all mysteries converge" (Henri de Lubac, *Meditación sobre la Iglesia*, Madrid 1988, 26). The Church is the place where all the mysteries meet, where they come together and illuminate each other: the mystery of the Trinity, of the Incarnation, of Redemption, of Grace, of the ultimate Realities.

The cosmic Temple

God begins to build this house when, with an absolutely free act of his Will, he determines to extend and share with other beings the dialogue of love that the Three divine Persons eternally exchange in the "silence of the eternal ages" that envelops them (cf. Rom 16:25). "If the heavenly Father were to cease uttering His Word, the effect of the Word, that is, the created universe, would not exist. In fact, what gives and preserves the being of the created universe is the Word (*locutio*) of God the Father, that is, the eternal and immutable Begetting of His Word" (John Scotus Eriugena, *Homélie sur le Prologue de Jean*, XVIII; SC 151, 288; PL 122, 293).

Being created in the image of the Son through the Father's act of love, every creature therefore receives, according to its capacity, the gift of praising God, and the whole cosmos thus becomes a preliminary model of the Church.

With the Creation of the cosmos God therefore laid the foundations of the Church, of the house where he would live his love story with us:

Do not think that I speak of the Bride and the Church only starting from the coming of the Saviour in the flesh, but rather I speak of it from the beginning of the human race and the very creation of the world; indeed, to climb higher to the origin of this mystery under the guidance of Paul, even before the creation of the world. (Origen, *In Canticum Canticorum*, II, 11, PG 13, 134)

The natural creation, the whole universe, this so to speak "cosmic" Church celebrates a true liturgy from the first moment of its existence, it prays already, because the cosmos, created in the image of the Son, in its silent language echoes the hymn of thanksgiving that the Son eternally raises to the Father in the silence of the Spirit.

With this "silent music" (St. John of the Cross, *Cantico Espiritual*, 15), in which "there is no speech, nor are there words" (cf. Ps 19:4), creation sings a prayer addressed to the Father, who recognizes in this silent praise an echo of the silence with which the Son welcomes the eternal word that begets him. As St. Gregory of Nazianzus sings:

All beings celebrate you,
the speaking and the mute.
The desire of the universe,
the groaning of all yearns for You.
All that is prays to You, and to You every being
that can read your universe raises a hymn of silence.
(*Hymn to God*, PG 37, 507–508)

God entrusted creation's hymn of silence to Adam so that he could decipher it, give it voice and sing it, giving it its true name. While creatures "by their mere existence … bless him and give him glory" (*CCC* 2416), man, created in a special way in the image of the Son, of him who was to come, of Christ (cf. Rom 5:14), could and should sing this hymn as an act of love, an act of thanksgiving, of "eucharist," deciphering in all creatures the image of him, of Christ who is the truth of creation. "With the bodily senses admire the beauty of sensible realities, and with the intellect discover in them the image of the Word of God" (John Scotus Eriugena, *op. cit.* XI; SC 151, 254; PL 122, 289). The whole universe, in fact, is the shadow of the Body of the Son (cf. Col 2:17), of him who, as Saint Paul says, "fills all in all" (Eph 1:23).

It is in the Liturgy that Creation rediscovers its original meaning of being the "body" of Christ. It is in the Liturgy that material creatures — bread, water, wine, oil, light — recover their original transparency and truly become the "epiphany" of Christ, and their groaning (Rom 8:22) is finally transformed into a song of praise to the Creator united with the Eucharistic song of Christ, in whom "the whole fullness of deity dwells bodily" (Col 2:9).

"We are his house" (Heb 3:6)

Begun with creation, the construction of this house of prayer comes to the final stage when the Father, with the Incarnation of the Son, places "as a foundation in Zion, a stone, a tested stone, a precious cornerstone, of a sure foundation" (Is 28:16). The "cornerstone" (Eph 2:20) that inseparably unites the two walls of the Temple: God and man. And then, as Saint Peter writes, "As you come to him, a living stone rejected by men but in the sight of God chosen and precious, you yourselves like living stones are being built up as a spiritual house, to be a holy priesthood, to offer spiritual sacrifices acceptable to God through Jesus Christ" (1 Pt 2:4–5).

It is therefore with the Incarnation of the Son, eternal Singer of the Father, that the song that "resounds eternally in the halls of heaven" is finally sung perfectly in our world too. Then God's desire to dwell with the sons of men is finally fulfilled (cf. Prv 8:31), because "by his Incarnation, he, the Son of God, *in a certain way united himself with each man* …without any exception whatever … *even when man is unaware of it*" (St. John Paul II, *Redemptor Hominis*, 13, 14, second emphasis added; cf. *Gaudium et Spes*, 22). To every man, without any exception, beyond his "merits" and his awareness, the Father has given the gift of oneness with Christ, the living stone, and thus of entering into the construction of the true Temple. In this way, with Christ, through Christ and in Christ, every man is now able to say to him, "Abba-Father," and thus participate in the eternal "song of praise that resounds in the halls of heaven."

Through this most intimate union that Christ establishes with every man, to the point that "now you are the body of Christ and individually members of it" (1 Cor 12:27), every man, each of us, is now destined not only to be a "man of prayer," but to "become prayer," as was said of Saint Francis, who "was not so much a man who prays, but rather was himself completely transformed into living prayer" (Thomas of Celano, *Second Life*, LXI, 95). We are destined to share fully in the very Mystery of the Son who in his very Person is prayer, is praise of the glory of the Father: "In him we have obtained an inheritance, having been predestined according to the purpose of him who works all things according to the counsel of his will, so that we who were the first to hope in Christ might be to the praise of his glory" (Eph 1:11–12). Being "praise of the Father's glory" is the sole and final destiny of every Christian and of the whole Church.

Adam, where are you? (Gen 3:9)

The Father is always looking to build his house. Even when we are unaware or are not thinking of him, he never neglects his work of "smoothing with chisel blows the stones fitted in place by a careful expert hand; they will always keep their place inside the sacred temple" (Dedication of a church, Hymn of Vespers). In every circumstance of our life he is present to make us living stones for his true Temple: the Body of Christ (cf. Jn 2:21). Through the little and big events that make up our day and our whole life, he is making us members of the Body of Christ, he is begetting the Son in the world. The events of our daily existence are "the talents" that he entrusts to us so that we can make them bear fruit, allowing his Spirit to mold us ever more into the image of the only Son. But, unfortunately, as we know, all too often we resist this incessant and silent work of God.

How can we discover in our daily life, so often murky, this incessant action of God who wants to give us the gift of prayer, wants to transform us into living stones of his house of prayer? God seeks each of us personally — "Where are you?" (Gn 3:9) — because "in calling Adam it is you that God calls" (Saint Ambrose, *Expositio in Psalmum 118*, I, 15; PL 15, 1206). But our response is too often the same as Adam's: "I heard the sound of you … and I was afraid … and I hid myself" (Gn 3:10).

Yet God is not resigned to losing man's love. He searches for him continually. As the Shepherd searches ravine and cliff for the sheep that has gone astray, so God "pursued the man who had fled from Him, and fled far away. And after pursuing him, He caught up to him and took him with Him. And He did so moved only by His goodness, by His charity and by the concern He has for us" (St. John Chrysostom, *In Epistolam ad Hebreos*, V, 1; PG 63, 46).

But too often our fear of Mystery paralyzes us and makes us reluctant before God's invitation:

You would like to lead me further, ever further, ever closer to the center, to the borders of your unknown kingdom. I understand, and it would be beautiful. You are patient; you wait for me at the lonely crossroads to teach me the way; you are truly discreet; you even make a show of fleeing from me, and you don't even dare to reveal your face. It would be beautiful, I know; I really want it. But my soul is deplorably shy; I scold it in vain; its wings tremble as soon as it is led towards the threshold of great adventures. … (D Buzzati, "Ombra del Sud," in *I Sette Messaggeri*, Milan, 1942, 74).

"*But behold, Thou wert close* on the steps of Thy fugitives, at once God of vengeance and Fountain of mercies, turning us to Thyself by wonderful means" (Saint Augustine, *Confessions*, IV, 4). In fact, "we seek God, while we are the ones sought. Our search is the fruit of a malaise that plants within us the pursuit — secret and untiring, gratuitous and unyielding — of a mercy whose face we do not know. To live with this certainty is to have crossed the threshold of the Gospel, it is to have accepted a Godward life." (Anonymous, *La Vie Spirituelle*, vol. 107, 1962, 229)

Allowing oneself to be built into a "house of God"

For this reason, the synthesis of the entire spiritual journey of every man, the heart of the journey of every prayer, is allowing oneself to be overtaken by the One who seeks us, to allow oneself to be touched by the hand of the Father who molds within us his only Son.

But due to our spiritual insensitivity it is often difficult to let ourselves be surprised by this God who seeks us incessantly and approaches us in an unexpected and surprising way. Our God is the "God in ambush" (F Mauriac, *Vie de Jésus*, Flammarion 1944, conclusion) who awaits us where we least expect him. So it was for Matthew, who was called while he was at the tax office, practicing an infamous profession (cf. Mt 9:9). Or as it was for Paul, dazzled by the Risen One on the road to Damascus, while he was going to persecute the Church (Acts 9:1).

The only way to discover this transforming action of the Father who continually seeks us is to nourish our desire for him. Jesus often weeps over us, as he wept over Jerusalem:

> "Would that you, even you, had known on this day the things that make for peace!" (Lk 19:42). And in words that have come down on papyrus, He gives voice to His lamentation over our insensitivity: "Jesus said, 'I was in the midst of the world and I saw them in flesh and bone, and I found them all drunk, and I found no one thirsty among them, and my soul is sorrowful for the sons of men, because they are blind of heart and do not see.'" (*Coptic Gospel of Thomas*, v. 28)

"I found no one thirsty … they are blind and do not see" … if we are not thirsty for God, we will not be able to see him or discover the gift he wants to offer us. Thirsting for God, thirsting to meet him … only this ardent desire for him, for his closeness, a desire that we must ask for like poor beggars from his Spirit, only this can open our eyes, can purify our gaze and thus allow us to see him, to "draw near to Him" in the only place where we can meet him: in his house of prayer, in the mystery of his Body, in his Church.

It is in the Song of Solomon, in this seeking, hiding and finding of the Bridegroom and the Bride, where we find described the whole journey of the Church's prayer. Prayer is the "place" where the Bridegroom and the Bride unite, where the two become one. Prayer is the "banqueting house" (Song 2:4) where the Bridegroom introduces the Bride to give himself to her, where the Church can say with full truth: "I am my beloved's and my beloved is mine" (Song 6:3; cf. 2:16).

Only with great spiritual modesty can we contemplate and try to speak of what happens in the secret intimacy of the Bridegroom and Bride.

Learning to Pray

We no longer know how to pray as we ought (cf. Rom 8:26)

So all of creation was oriented towards being "house of God and house of prayer," and the priest of this Church was "Adam, the son of God" (Lk 3:38), created in the image and likeness of the Son so that he could be, like the Son, a song of praise and thanksgiving to the Father.

The response of our first parents, who did not want to *receive* the gift of divine Life as the Son *receives* it but wanted to gain independent mastery of it, brought a terrible dimming, in them and in us, of the light that allowed them to see and praise God in themselves and in the creation that surrounded them. They almost completely lost the capacity to give voice to creation's hymn of praise. And this song of the universe that told of the Glory of God (cf. Ps 19:1) became a feeble voice, imperceptible to the ears of the man who had preferred to listen to another voice, that of the Adversary.

And from then on, the song of creation changed

into groaning (cf. Rom 8:22).

But the worst consequence of the first sin was the deformation of the image of God in our first parents, a deformation that created an almost insurmountable obstacle to prayer. Intimacy with God, which before sin was man's joy, has now turned into fear. At the approach of God, Adam hid: "I was afraid ... and I hid myself" (Gn 3:10) ... and we with him.

And even now we continue to hide, to leave unanswered God's desire to be with us. We are afraid of intimacy with him, because it is in prayer that the image of God in our hearts is revealed to us. And this image is a caricature carved into us by the lying voice of the Adversary, who insinuated, "God does not want you to be gods, God does not want you to be like Him" (cf. Gn 3:5). Ultimately he was implying, "God is not as good as He seems. God is not what He has shown you. He has another face. His true face is that of a master." And this lie has been imprinted so deeply in our mind and spirit that we don't even realize it.

This caricature of God is the idol we often serve with our prayer. Many, too many times, we have thought that prayer is our "duty," a duty of the creature, of the man who must give worship to God, to the Sovereign of all things, to the Master of our lives, to an inaccessible God, to a God deaf to our sufferings and our desires, who steers our lives as he pleases, according to his inscrutable plan.

We must recognize with painful sincerity that this

is the image of God that has always accompanied our prayer, and makes it so wearisome and "alien" to our heart. "For we do not know what to pray for as we ought" (Rom 8:26). In fact, often, all too often, we are praying to an idol that wants us as slaves.

But God did not let himself be "discouraged" by all this … he continued to seek after Adam: "Adam, where are you?" (Gn 3:9). He did not want to give up on his dream of their life together. And he continued to build the house where he could be with him. He continued to build his Church:

> The Holy Church, which was promised as a bride at the beginning of the world in paradise, was prefigured in the flood, was proclaimed through the Law, was designated by means of the prophets, long awaited the splendor of the Gospel, the redemption of men, the coming of her Beloved. (Saint Ambrose, *Expositio in Psalmum 118*, 1; PL 15, 1201)

"Lord, teach us to pray!" (Lk 11:1)

But now, with the Incarnation of the Word, the beloved has come, the Bridegroom has descended into his garden (cf. Song 5:1) and with him "the winter is past … the time of singing has come" (Song 2:11–12). Now the Son has *"introduced into this earthly exile that hymn which is sung throughout all ages in the halls of heaven."* In our universe and in the heart of man rendered mute by sin and incapable of praising the Father as he ought, Christ, with the whole of his human life, introduces the eternal song that he, moved by the Spirit, sings "in the halls of heaven": "Abba-Father."

A song that only he can sing in truth and that only the little ones of the earth can learn: "[Jesus] rejoiced in the *Holy Spirit* and said, 'I thank you, *Father*, Lord of heaven and earth, that you have hidden these things from the wise and understanding and revealed them to little children'" (Lk 10:21; emphasis added).

This song, "Abba," was the longing of God himself: "I thought you would call me, My Father, / and would not turn from following me. / Surely, as a treacherous wife leaves her husband, / so have you been treacherous to me" (Jer 3:19–20). "Why, when I came, was there no man; / why when I called, was there no one to answer?" (Is 50:2). And, "Let them make peace with me, / let them make peace with me" (Is 27:5).

This song was the longing of Adam; it was the song that, after his exile from paradise, he could now no longer sing.

This song was the desire of the prophets and the Psalmist, who could listen to it only "from afar," in faith. In fact, "These all died in faith, not having received the things promised, but having seen them and greeted them from afar, and having acknowledged that they were strangers and exiles on the earth" (Heb 11:13).

They glimpsed it because, after Adam's sin, this song

of the Son was entrusted by the Father to "his son" (Hos 11:11; Dt 14:1; Ps 82:6), to the people of Israel. And Israel sang it and made it resound in the psalms, in the law and in the prophets. And the beauty of the words of the law, the prophets and the psalms came to them because it was an echo of this song.

But it was a song that was expressed "in a mirror dimly" (1 Cor 13:12). Israel could really contemplate God in the words of this song, "it saw the Word" (Ex 20:18, Vulgate), but as "behind a veil," because "only through Christ is [the veil] taken away" (2 Cor 3:14). So when one of his disciples said to him, "Lord, teach us to pray" (Lk 11:1), Jesus turned to the disciples in private and said, "Blessed are the eyes that see what you see! For I tell you that many prophets and kings desired to see what you see, and did not see it, *and to hear what you hear, and did not hear it*" (Lk 10:21–24, emphasis added).

On an extraordinary page, Clement of Alexandria explains what this new song consisted of and who sang it:

And He who is of David, and yet before him, the Word of God, despising the lyre and harp, which are but lifeless instruments, and having tuned by the Holy Spirit the universe, and especially man — who, composed of body and soul, is a universe in miniature — makes melody to God on this instrument of many tones. … What, then, does this instrument — the Word of God, the Lord, the new song — desire? To open the eyes of the blind, and unstop the ears of the deaf, and to lead the lame or the erring to righteousness, to exhibit God to the foolish, to put a stop to corruption, to conquer death, to reconcile disobedient children to their father. The instrument of God loves mankind. ... For, according to that inspired apostle of the Lord, 'the grace of God which brings salvation has appeared to all men' (Ti 2:11). This is the new song, the manifestation of the Word that was in the beginning, and before the beginning. ... He did not now for the first time pity us for our error; but He pitied us from the first, from the beginning. But now, at His appearance, lost as we already were, He accomplished our salvation. (*Exhortation to the Heathen*, ch. 1; PG 8, 55–62)

The harp of the cross

Jesus sang this "new song" throughout his life, but in a full and perfect way when, accompanying himself with the harp of the cross, he said, "Father, into your hands I commit my spirit" (Cf. Saint Bonaventure, *Vitis Mystica*, 8:31; 15:49; PL 184, 655, 665):

When the time comes to pass from this world to the Father (Jn 13:1), with all His being Jesus rises towards God, He himself becomes prayer, He, the Son who is entirely bent upon God. *The Passover*

*of death and resurrection is the mystery of Jesus be-
come prayer.* (FX Durrwell, *Lo Spirito Santo alla
Luce del Mistero Pasquale*, Rome 1985, 73)

It is there, in this act of donation unto death and without reservation, where the Son "says" perfectly, in human categories, with truly human acts and words, what
he says ineffably in the bosom of the eternal Trinity:
"Abba, Father, I give myself without reservation to You;
into your hands I commit my spirit."

> In his last words on the Cross ... prayer and
> the gift of self are but one" (*CCC* 2605). For "the
> mystery of the glorious Cross is the Trinitari-
> an mystery brought into the world. Only in the
> glorious death of Jesus, and nowhere else, is the
> Spirit thus present in the world; never before was
> the Spirit given in the way in which He is poured
> forth in this glorious death: "As yet the Spirit had
> not been given, because Jesus was not yet glori-
> fied" (Jn 7:39). (cf. FX Durrwell, *El Espíritu San-
> to en La Iglesia*, Salamanca 1990, 55–65)

Now that Jesus is "glorified" (cf. Jn 12:23 *et passim*),
that is, with the utmost gift of himself "to the point
of death, even death on a cross" (Phil 2:8), has shown
who he really is, has fully revealed the mystery of his
Person, his being the Son "who through the eternal
Spirit offered himself without blemish to God" (Heb
9:14), to the Father, only now can the Spirit in whom

Jesus eternally says "Abba" pour himself forth in our world and teach us the true prayer, "Abba."

This is the mystery that John contemplated *in symbolo* on Calvary, and that so "shocked" him as to make him affirm almost with an oath that "he who saw it has borne witness — his testimony is true, and he knows that he tells the truth — that you also may believe" (Jn 19:35). And this same mystery was later shown to him in Revelation, where he saw "without veil" the reality of what had happened on Golgotha:

> And I saw the holy city, new Jerusalem, coming down out of heaven from God, prepared as a bride adorned for her husband And I heard a loud voice from the throne saying, 'Behold, the dwelling place of God is with man.' To the thirsty I will give from the spring of the water of life without payment. The one who conquers will have this heritage, and I will be his God and he will be my son. (Revelation 21:2–3, 6–7)

The Spirit, Master of prayer
"Praying in the Holy Spirit" (Jude 1:20)

The pierced side of the Paschal Body of Jesus, of his crucified and risen Body, from which "immediately" gush forth "water and blood," is the only wellspring of the Spirit. And the Spirit is the One who teaches us to pray, because "God has sent the Spirit of his Son into our hearts, crying, 'Abba! Father!'" (Gal 4:6). He, "[interceding] for us with groanings too deep for words"

(Rom 8:26), makes up for our inability to pray as we ought (ibid).

The Spirit, "hovering" (Gn 1:1) over the Water and Blood that flowed from the right side of the true Temple (cf. Ez 47:1; Jn 2:21, 19:34), begins the new creation, the Church, the new Jerusalem, born of the Water of Baptism and the Blood of the Eucharist.

> At the same moment in which a soldier opened the side of Christ, there immediately came out blood and water, which spread to give life to the world.
>
> The side of Christ is the life of the world, the side of the second Adam (cf. 1 Cor 15:45). The side of Christ is the life of the Church. ... Behold now Eve, mother of all the living. The mother of the living is the Church that God has built, placing Christ as the cornerstone (cf. Eph 2:20). Now the Woman is created, now she is formed, now she is built up and takes shape. Now the spiritual House is raised for a holy priesthood (1 Pt 2:5).
>
> Come, Lord, form this Woman, build the City. Behold the Woman, mother of all, behold the spiritual House, behold the City that lives eternally because it does not know death. (Saint Ambrose, *In Lucam*, II, 86–88; PL 15, 1584–1585)

From the cross there now gushes living Water, and "if anyone thirst, let him come to me and drink" (Jn 7:37).

"Come, everyone who thirsts, come to the waters; and he who has no money, come" (Is 55:1), because "To the thirsty I will give from the spring of the water of life without payment" (Rv 21:6). "And all were made to drink of one Spirit" (1 Cor 12:13), because the Wellspring "thirsts to be thirsted for" (St. Gregory Nazianzen, *Oration XL*, 36, 397), thirsts to be drunk.

The Spirit, therefore, in quenching believers, in uniting them with the oblation of Jesus on the cross, gives them, by this very fact, the gift of the pinnacle of prayer, of being able to say with Jesus and like Jesus, "Abba, Father." He gives them the ability to share the Son's relationship with the Father. The Spirit, in giving us the prayer of Jesus, "immerses" us, "baptises" us into the very life of the Trinity (cf. Mt 28:19).

"The Holy Spirit raises the soul in a sublime manner so that she will accomplish in God the same spiration of love that the Father spirates in the Son and the Son in the Father, and is the Holy Spirit himself" (St. John of the Cross, *Cántico Espiritual A*, stanza 38).

In fact, "because you are sons, God has sent the Spirit of his Son into our hearts, crying, 'Abba! Father!'" (Gal 4:6).

As one monk has written:

The discovery of God as our Father is, it seems to me, a spiritual attainment beyond which one cannot go, because it allows access in the most direct way possible into the experience of Christ himself, both as eternal Son and as Man and

34

Redeemer. It has always seemed to me that one cannot go any further, and that such great peace (like that which flows from abandonment to the Father) cannot be equaled by anything else, not even by spiritual marriage. If we can truly say "my Father" with complete trust, we will have found our deep identity, we will become, in a certain sense, "indifferent" to everything else. Because nothing that can happen in life can touch us more deeply than this word: "My Father."

Now, prayer can be authentic only if it is united with that of Jesus on the cross, and with him "cries." "Abba, Father, into your hands I commit my spirit."

But in order to say "Father" with Christ and as He says it:

We must humbly cleanse our hearts of certain false images. … The purification of our hearts has to do with paternal or maternal images, stemming from our personal and cultural history, and influencing our relationship with God. God our Father transcends the categories of the created world. To impose our own ideas in this area 'upon him' would be to fabricate idols to adore or pull down. (*CCC* 2779)

This path of purification, necessary for each of us, is a path of great poverty, but above all of great sincerity, and only a true desire to "see the Face of God" can sustain us on this path of purification of the heart.

The "vision" of God is the beatitude that Jesus promised to the pure of heart, but the deformed image of God revealed in "our" prayer tells us that our heart is not "pure," unable to receive only love and give only love, in poverty. Left only to itself and its dynamics, our heart inevitably seeks only what it knows, building relationships, including that with God (especially that with God) out of the "material" that its personal history has placed at its disposal, and it cannot be otherwise. And parental images are a central element of this inner world of ours, the foundation on which we set the construction of our relationships with the external world: with others and with God himself.

This is why it is necessary that the grace of the Spirit, which teaches Jesus to say "Father," should also teach us to say it with Jesus in the same way and with the same meaning. Or rather, that it be He himself, the Spirit, who says it in us, making us one with Christ: "Have this mind among yourselves, which is yours in Christ Jesus" (Phil 2:5).

And the sentiments of Christ Jesus are those of the Son, sentiments that, translated into human language, correspond to what is called "childhood." Because childhood is not, as we often romantically suppose, the age of innocence. Children are often cruel and selfish. What is proper to childhood is its absolute poverty. A small child cannot be self-sufficient. Left to himself, he dies. He has a vital need for the care of others.

This is why Jesus solemnly states that only "he who

welcomes the kingdom of God as a child does will enter into it" (cf. Lk 18:17; Mk 10:15). And a child "knows" that he cannot do anything on his own, that he needs everything and everyone.

Only when the Spirit has made our hearts so poor as to make our own the Son's cry of supplication (Mk 14:36), of being aware of having an extreme need of grace, only then can we truly say with Jesus and as He does: "Abba, Papa, I need You. Without You I can do nothing."

For this reason we will truly be children, and will thus be able to fully welcome the gift of the Kingdom, the gift of true prayer, only when we allow ourselves to be crucified by the humiliation of not knowing how and not being able to live this new life of the Kingdom by our own power.

The acceptance of our personal, physical, psychological and moral poverty is the only means by which we can receive the Divine glory and bear witness to its presence already within us. Accepted with humility and trust, this perpetual poverty of ours becomes the setting and means by which to say "Abba!" to God. It becomes our death, it becomes our Passover, our daily passage to the Father and our resurrection.

Precisely for this reason, our daily experience of a weakness that never comes to an end disposes us to live in total dependence on the mercy of the Father, to receive everything, literally everything, from him. As it was for Jesus, "who offered prayers and supplications to God, who was able to save him from death, and because of his total abandonment to Him was heard" (cf. Heb 5:7), and was saved from death precisely by means of death, so will it be for us too. The Father will save us from our poverty and misery only when we accept that we cannot free ourselves from it on our own.

"The weaker we are, without desire and without virtue, the more suited we are for the operations of this Love that consumes and transforms! ... But we must agree to remain poor and without strength, and this is the difficult thing," St. Thérèse of the Child Jesus boldly writes (Letter of September 17, 1896, *Complete Works*, Rome 1997, 538).

Like the Son, the sacrificed and risen Lamb, we too will bear our wounds eternally, a sign of our weakness and our death. But above all a sign of our resurrection. Because as it was for him, so also for us it is through our wounds that the Glory of the Father has been able to be poured out into our flesh and into our lives:

> How then shall we glorify God for so great a gift? God cannot be glorified by us in a manner different from how He was glorified by His Son. The ways by which the Son has glorified the Father are the same by which the Father has glorified the Son. These ways pass through the cross, that is, through death to the whole world, through the afflictions, temptations and other sufferings of Christ. If we endure these things with great

patience, we imitate the suffering Christ and thus glorify our Father and our God, as His children by grace, we who are co-heirs with Christ. (Symeon the New Theologian, *Practical and Theological Chapters* 101; PG 120, 658–659)

Love to the point of giving one's life, "to the end" (Jn 13:1) is the "new song" that the bridegroom teaches his bride. It is the song that Christ has given to his Church, as St. Paul VI said. This is the song that is sung by those who follow the Lamb *wherever* he goes, who do not ask him "where" he is going, but simply follow him, looking only at him, contemplating only him, not letting their loving gaze swerve from him:

I am not asking you now to think of Him, or to form numerous conceptions of Him, or to make long and subtle meditations with your understanding. I am asking you only to look at Him. … See, He is only waiting for us to look at Him, as He says to the Bride (St. Teresa of Jesus, *Camino de Perfección*, 26, 3, in *Obras Completas*, Madrid, 1954, 195–196).

Contemplation is a gaze of faith, fixed on Jesus. 'I look at him and he looks at me': this is what a certain peasant of Ars used to say to his holy curé about his prayer before the tabernacle. This focus on Jesus is a renunciation of self. His gaze purifies our heart." (*CCC* 2715)

This gaze of faith and love is the song of the Bride:

> You have captivated my heart, my sister, my bride;
> you have captivated my heart with one glance of
> your eyes. (Song 4:9)

It is the "new song that the redeemed sing before the throne and before the four living creatures and the elders. And no one could understand that song except the … redeemed from the earth" (Rv 14:3).

The Song of the Bride

———

The Liturgy

O my dove, in the clefts of the rock,
    in the crannies of the cliff,
let me see your face,
    let me hear your voice. (Song 2:14)

The desire of the Lamb is to sing his "new song" to the Father in unison with us, to unite us so intimately with himself that his voice can be heard in us and ours in him (cf. Saint Augustine, *Enarrationes in Psalmos*, Ps 85; PL 37, 108).

With the gift of his Spirit, he has made us one with him, one Body, "we are members of his body" (Eph 5:30) like the bride with the groom. As in the nuptial union "a man shall leave his father and his mother and hold fast to his wife, and they shall become one flesh" (Gn 2:24; Eph 5:31), so also Christ does with those who unite with him through faith. Christ "left" the Father, experiencing his silence and atrocious absence on the cross, in order to be able to unite with his bride. And from the cross Jesus draws everyone and everything to himself to form with them one flesh, one body that lives just one life, his own. For this reason, St. Leo the Great would be able to affirm that "the body of the baptized becomes the flesh of Christ" (*Sermon LXIII*, 6; PL 54, 357). "This mystery is profound, and I am saying that it refers to Christ and the church" (Eph 5:32). The Church is born on the Paschal cross, and there she celebrates her nuptial union with her Bridegroom.

As a nuptial dowry, as a pledge of his love and union, Christ gave her himself in an act of offering, his own Act of offering that perfectly glorifies the Father. He gave her the gift of his prayer, of himself become prayer.

We receive this gift in the Liturgy, because the Liturgy "is also a participation in Christ's own prayer addressed to the Father in the Holy Spirit. In the liturgy, *all Christian prayer* finds its source and goal" (*CCC* 1073, emphasis added), even the most intimate and secret prayer, the most silent and hidden, that which only "the Father who is in secret" (Mt 6:6) can hear. Because if it is certainly true that "the spiritual life ... is not limited solely to participation in the liturgy ... the Christian ... must also enter into his chamber to pray to the Father, in secret" (*Sacrosanctum Concilium*, 12), it is no less true that only union with the prayer of Christ, sacramentally present in the Liturgy, can release "our" prayer.

In fact, this participation in the prayer of Christ, in his offering to the Father, is not a simple devout remembrance of Jesus. If it were so, Jesus would essentially be just a great moral teacher, an admirable model, a great holy man, and his presence among us would be equal to that of a great philosopher among his pupils:

> If the resurrection were for us a concept, an idea, a thought; if the Risen One were for us the recollection of the recollection of others, however authoritative, as, for example, of the apostles; if there were not given also to us the possibility of a true encounter with him, that would be to declare the newness of the Word-made-Flesh to have been all used up. Instead, the Incarnation, in addition to being the only always new event that history knows, is also the very method that the Holy Trinity has chosen to open to us the way of communion. Christian faith is either an encounter with him alive, or it does not exist.

> The Liturgy guarantees for us the possibility of such an encounter. For us a vague memory of the Last Supper would do no good. We need to be present at that Supper, to be able to hear his voice, to eat his Body and to drink his Blood. We need Him. (Pope Francis, *Desiderio Desideravi*, 10–11)

In fact,

> no one can understand the liturgy until he has grasped the fact that Christ is present in it not as an abstract idea but as a living person and as a living force emanating from a living person: "and therefore He can assure perfect salvation to those who approach God through Him, as He is always alive to intercede on their behalf" (Heb 7:25) and to act through them and with them.
>
> In the liturgy, Christ's priestly action becomes really present for us. Time is surpassed and, as it were, suspended: Christ, His sacrifice, His sanctifying power, His prayer, are present, really, physically, under the veil of signs. Thus all men throughout the ages become contemporaries of Christ by participating in the liturgy; not that they escape time and space to return to the time of Christ; but Christ, always living and present, draws them into the orbit of His priestly action, which henceforth transcends space and time. (Cipriano Vagaggini, *Theological Dimensions of the Liturgy*, Liturgical Press, Collegeville 1959, 148)

What makes this possible is Christ's Paschal mystery:

> [This is] the unique event of history which does not pass away: Jesus dies, is buried, rises from the dead, and is seated at the right hand of the Father "once for all" (Rom 6:10; Heb 7:27; 9:12; cf. Jn

13:1; 17:1). His Paschal mystery is a real event that occurred in our history, but it is unique: all other historical events happen once, and then they pass away, swallowed up in the past. The Paschal mystery of Christ, by contrast, cannot remain only in the past, because by his death he destroyed death, and all that Christ is — all that he did and suffered for all men — participates in the divine eternity, and so transcends all times while being made present in them all. The event of the Cross and Resurrection abides and draws everything towards life. (*CCC* 1085)

The Eucharist, the wedding banquet of the Lamb (cf. Rv 19:9)

This union and identification with Christ in his priestly act of presenting himself to the Father, "a fragrant offering and sacrifice to God" (Eph 5:2), reaches its summit in the sacramental union of the Eucharist, in the wedding banquet that the Father has prepared for his Son and to which he has invited everyone, poor, "maimed, blind and lame, good and bad" (cf. Mt 22:2–10; Lk 14:21).

The "difficult" words that He spoke at the synagogue of Capernaum, Jesus asks us to listen to and believe literally, with simplicity of spirit and with the faith of little children:

Truly, truly, I say to you, unless you eat the flesh of the Son of Man and drink his blood, you have no life in you. Whoever feeds on my flesh and drinks my blood has eternal life, and I will raise him up on the last day. For my flesh is true food, and my blood is true drink. Whoever feeds on my flesh and drinks my blood abides in me, and I in him. As the living Father sent me, and I live because of the Father, so whoever feeds on me, he also will live because of me. (John 6:53–57)

"Whoever feeds on me, he also will live because of me." … In this wedding banquet the Bridegroom unites himself so intimately with the Bride as to make himself her food and drink and become her life, so that the two may live just one life, that of the Bridegroom.

Nicholas Kabasilas comments with enthusiasm:

> When He takes him to the sacred Table and gives him His Body to eat, Christ changes the initiate completely and changes his way of being. When the clay receives the royal form, it ceases to be clay and becomes the body of the King. Nothing happier than this can be conceived! Indeed, our soul is united with His soul, our body with His body and our blood with His blood. As Paul comments about the resurrection, "The mortal is swallowed up in life." And he adds, "I live, but it is no longer I, but rather Christ lives in me." (*Life in Christ*, IV, I, 2, 3, 6, 7, 8; PG 150, 583–586)

This mysterious incorporation, which took place once and for all in our Baptism, with which we have been made co-corporeal with Christ, becomes almost visible in the Eucharist because, according to the word of the Lord, "Whoever feeds on my flesh and drinks my blood abides in me, and I in him" (Jn 6:56). Here, as an ancient council states, "This mystery of unity reaches perfection, because we receive from Him what He received from us" (Lateran Council IV, canon 1 *de Fide catholica*). We receive from Christ the Body that He received from the Virgin Mary. There his Body is "completed" as ours is united with his, and therefore in a certain sense Christ "is born" because he becomes ever more visible.

In the liturgy, above all in the Eucharist, Christ, uniting the Church to himself, is mysteriously completing his Body as bit by bit men cleave to him by faith:

> This communication of the Spirit of Christ is the channel through which all the gifts, powers, and extra-ordinary graces found superabundantly in the Head as in their source flow into all the members of the Church. ... Thus the Church becomes, as it were, the filling out and the complement of the Redeemer. (Pius XII, *Mystici Corporis*, 77)

In the Eucharist, through Christ, with Christ and in Christ, our perfect union with the Trinity is realized, the Church reaches its fullness and according to the bold expression of Tertullian, it becomes "the body of the Three" (*de Baptismo*, VI; PL 1, 1206), the visible manifestation of the mystery of love that constitutes the Life of God.

The Divine Office

In the Eucharistic Liturgy, therefore, Christ truly unites us "corporeally" to his "new song." The Eucharist is the summit of our union with Christ in his prayer of praise to Father. But precisely because it is its summit, it configures the life of the faithful to itself and expands throughout the whole. There is a "place" where this influence of the Eucharist is particularly intense, where it extends itself and "molds," so to speak, the prayer of the Church. It is the Divine Office, where the voice of the Bride and that of the Bridegroom merge into a single voice, where the complete Body of Christ, Head and members, sings his own Word to the Father with one voice:

> He joins the entire community of mankind to himself, associating it with His own singing of this canticle of divine praise.
>
> For he continues His priestly work through the agency of His Church, which is ceaselessly engaged in praising the Lord and interceding for the salvation of the whole world. She does this, not only by celebrating the eucharist, but also in other ways, especially by praying the divine office. ...
>
> It is truly the voice of the bride addressed

to her bridegroom; it is the very prayer which Christ himself, together with His body, addresses to the Father.

Hence all who render this service are not only fulfilling a duty of the Church, but also are sharing in the greatest honor of Christ's spouse, for by offering these praises to God they are standing before God's throne in the name of the Church their Mother." (*Sacrosanctum Concilium*, 83–85)

They are the immense multitude, which no one could count, of every nation, tribe, people and tongue. All stood before the throne and before the Lamb, clothed in white robes, and they held palm branches in their hands. They sing the song of the Lamb, a new song, before the throne and before the four living creatures and the elders (cf. Rv 7:9; 14:3; 15:3).

Like Christ, who has no words of his own but says only what he has heard from the Father (cf. Jn 12:50), so too the Church has no words of her own. She can sing only the song of the Lamb slain and risen, the song that her Bridegroom has taught her. It is Christ who speaks in the words of the Church,

because Christ is in the members of Christ. And that you may know that Head and members together are one Christ, He himself says, speaking of marriage: they will be two in one flesh, therefore no longer two, but one flesh. ... In the prophet Isaiah He calls himself "bridegroom and bride" (cf. Is 61:10). Why does He say He is Bridegroom and Bride, if not because they will be two in one flesh? If two in one flesh, why not two in one voice? Let Christ therefore speak, since in Christ the Church speaks and in the Church Christ speaks: and the Body in the Head and the Head in the Body. … For this reason He also says in the Gospel: I am the vine, you are the branches, my Father is the vinedresser; and adds: without me you can do nothing. Yes, O Lord, nothing without you, but everything in you. For everything He does through us, it seems that we are the ones doing it. In truth He can do much, everything, even without us: we nothing without Him. (Saint Augustine, *Enarrationes in Psalmos*; PL 36, 231–232)

As Benedict XVI explains, "In Baptism we surrender ourselves, we place our lives in his hands, and so we can say with Saint Paul, 'It is no longer I who live, but Christ who lives in me'" (Easter Vigil homily, 2007). "Thus the Church's prayer is Christ's prayer, and Christ's prayer is the Church's" (C. Vagaggini, *op. cit.* 147). And to be able to be associated with the song of praise that the Son raises to the Father in the eternal silence of Trinity is the beatitude of the Church, our beatitude: "Blessed are those who dwell in your house, / ever singing your praise" (Ps 84:4).

In the singing of the Liturgy of the Hours it is the Church of all times and places that sings. As Blessed Cardinal Schuster confided:

[When I pray the Office,] I close my eyes, and while my lips murmur the words of the Breviary that I know entirely by heart, I leave their literal meaning behind to feel myself in the endless wasteland where the pilgrim and militant Church makes its way, journeying towards the promised homeland. I draw breath with the Church in the same light by day, in the same darkness by night; I mark on every side the hosts of evil that threaten or attack it; I find myself in the midst of its battles and its victories, its prayers of anguish and its songs of triumph, the oppression of prisoners, the groans of the dying, the rejoicing of the armies and victorious captains. I find myself in the midst of this: not as a passive spectator, but rather as a participant whose watchfulness, dexterity, strength and courage can have a decisive impact on the fate of the struggle between good and evil and on the eternal destinies of individuals and of the multitude. (G Colombo, Novissima Verba, in *Scritti del Cardinale Alfredo Ildefonso Schuster*, Venegono Inferiore 1959, 23–33)

The Liturgy of the Heart:
the Life of Prayer

The desire for God: unceasing prayer

"[It is necessary] always to pray and not lose heart." (Luke 18:1)

"Pray without ceasing." (1 Thessalonians 5:17)

The words of Jesus in Saint Luke and of Saint Paul to the Thessalonians have always been the point of reference that have indicated to the Church and to every Christian the need for unceasing prayer. One form of this unceasing prayer is without a doubt the Liturgy of the Hours, in which, as has been seen, the Church preserves *with constancy and faithfulness the song of praise that Jesus Christ the High Priest introduced into this land of exile.*

But even if it is absolutely necessary, union with Christ in the Liturgy alone is not enough if it does not become the stable form of our entire life. We must give to Christ without reservation our whole person, soul and body, all our desires and sentiments, good and bad, in order to receive from him what is ours transfigured into what is his, so that our sentiments may be transformed into the same sentiments of Christ (cf. Phil 2:5), as Saint Paul asks of us. In the end we must give him our whole life so that he may continue to live his life in us, so that he may pray ceaselessly within us, repeat within us: "Abba."

But our abandonment to him, even if we sincerely want it to be complete, is unfortunately always partial. We are always holding something back, there is in us always a mixture of true love for God and reluctance to abandon ourselves without reservation to him. This is why it takes all of our life and all of our death so that the Word may take full possession of our person, of our body and our soul, so that he may become flesh in us.

Only the desire to be united with Jesus, so that our life may become so to speak interchangeable with his and his with ours, is what can allow us to live in unceasing prayer. We must constantly return to him; we must look at him again when we realize that we have dropped our gaze from him. We must accept dying to ourselves so that he can live in us. And this death must embrace our entire person, even the most hidden corners of our heart. Nothing of our person must escape this "invasion" of Christ, on pain of "remaining in death" (cf. 1 Jn 3:14) because, in the words of St. Gregory of Nazianzus, "what [Christ] has not assumed He has not healed" (*Epistola 101*; PG 37, 182–183).

We must give him everything, the little light and the much darkness, the good and the evil that is in us, so that Christ may heal all that is ours and all that is ours may become Christ's. It is a true death, and frightening. But it is the heart of our Christian and monastic vocation.

In Jeremiah, God speaks a word that realistically describes all of this. The Lord asks, "Who would dare of himself to approach me?" (Jer 30:21).

"He who is near me is near fire," says a word of Jesus handed down by the Fathers (Didymus the blind, *Expositio in Psalmos*, 88, 8; PG 39, 1487). He who prays wants to be near the fire, despite knowing that the fire will burn him. He prefers to be consumed by this nearness; he prefers the humiliation and pain of these burns rather than being removed from Christ, even just a little, because he knows that "he who is far from fire is far from the Kingdom," as the word of Jesus continues (ibid.).

Agreeing that Jesus should live within us his life, his offering to the Father, his prayer, "Abba," means agreeing to risk our life. Mary fully accepted this risk, and this is why she is the creature closest to God. We too, with Baptism, have accepted this risk of "being" with him (cf. Mk 3:14).

Perhaps we did not grasp or understand all the consequences. Perhaps we did not know that the risk was so great. But we accepted. We agreed to be close to Jesus. We did not think that there would be such a total collapse of all we had within us, of all our certainties, all our ideas, all our dreams. But little by little, as we have gone along, God has revealed it to us. It is only the Spirit who gives us the strength to take the risk that comes from the intimacy of life with Christ. To "abandon oneself to the Gospel," as Madeleine Delbrêl put it, "it is necessary to immerse oneself in death, in universal frailty, in the actual decomposition of all values, of human groups and of ourselves. ... One must know one is lost in order to want to be saved" (*Nous Autres, Gens des Rues*, Paris, 1966, 79). And it is by grace that, day after day, we place in the hands of the Lord what still remains of ourselves ... desiring that ever less of us remain, so that he may be ever more the whole of our life.

This desire for him, which is his grace, is our prayer. And if the desire is not broken off, we are always at prayer. In a famous page, Saint Augustine speaks of this prayer of desire:

> If your desire is before Him, the Father, who sees in secret, will grant it. Your desire is your prayer: if your desire is continuous, continuous also is your prayer. The Apostle, in fact, does not say by chance, "Pray without ceasing" (1 Thes 5:17). Does this perhaps mean that we must remain on our knees or prostrate or with hands raised to

obey the command to pray constantly? If this is our understanding of prayer, I maintain that we cannot do this without interruption. But there is another kind of prayer, interior, which is without interruption, and that is desire. Whatever you may do, if you desire that Sabbath (which is repose in God), you never stop praying. If you do not want to let up praying, do not stop desiring. Your desire is continuous, continuous is your voice. You will fall silent if you cease to love. The coldness of love is the silence of the heart, the ardour of love is the cry of the heart. If love remains ever alive, you cry out always; if you cry out always, you always desire; if you desire, you have your thoughts turned towards peace. "In you rests all my hope" (Ps 38:9). (*Enarrationes in Psalmos,* Ps 34, 14; PL 36, 404)

The prayer of the Church is unceasing because the Bride is always, unceasingly, longing for her Bridegroom.

Thirst

> … my soul thirsts for you.
> my flesh faints for you,
>> as like a dry and weary land where there is no
>> water. (Psalm 63:1)

But even though our heart thirsts for life, for a life that never ends, for a perfect life, and we "know" where to find it, since Adam we have sought this life outside of

God and far from God. As he himself says, complaining to the prophet Jeremiah, "they have forsaken me, / the fountain of living waters, / and hewed out cisterns for themselves, / broken cisterns that can hold no water" (Jer 2:13). Where we think there is water, we try to quench our thirst for life by digging out cracked cisterns. But we end up more and more disappointed and thirsty because, in the best-case scenario, what we succeed in finding is only stagnant, bitter water.

But God "thirsts for our thirst" (St. Gregory Nazianzen, *Oration XL*; PG 36, 397) much more than we can thirst for him, because he knows that without him we cannot live. Created in his image and likeness, in the image of him who is life itself, we have lost this likeness, and from this point on our life is just a slow death. So God himself has set out to look for us, lost and wandering sheep. God knows that only his Love in person can quench our thirst. He came to offer us life, so that we might have his life and have it in abundance (cf. Jn 10:10). And this Life is in the Son, "who came by water and blood" (1 Jn 5:6).

The prophet Ezekiel ends his book with an arresting vision of God's lifegiving water:

Water was issuing from below the threshold of the temple towards the east … and the water was flowing down from below the south end of the threshold of the temple. … And he said to me, "This water flows towards the eastern region and goes down into the Arabah; and enters the sea; when the water flows into the sea, the water will become fresh. And wherever the river goes every living creature that swarms will live … for this water goes there, that the waters of the sea may become fresh; so everything will live where the river goes. … And on the banks, on both sides of the river, there will grow all kinds of trees for food. Their leaves will not wither nor their fruit fail, but they will bear fresh fruit every month, because the water for them flows from the sanctuary. Their fruit will be for food, and their leaves for healing." (Ezekiel 47:1–12)

This river of Living Water flowed from the south side of the true Temple when "one of the soldiers pierced his side with a spear, and at once there came out blood and water" (Jn 19:34). From the cross, from the throne where the Lamb, slain and glorified, is perfectly united with the Father (cf. Rv 5:6), arises this river (Rv 22:1) to give life to the world, to quench the thirst of God and our thirst. And since then this river has not stopped gushing forth and pouring out onto the earth.

The Spirit is poured out and acts in the depths of hearts, drawing them secretly and powerfully towards the Wellspring from which he himself flows, towards the Heart of Christ and the Heart of the Father. As St. Ignatius of Antioch said, "There is living water within me that speaks to me, saying, Come to the Father"

(*Letter to the Romans*, VII).

The Spirit arouses and keeps alive in our hearts this thirst for living water, this longing for the Face of the *true* God.

And there was a moment in which we "saw" the face of God, and it was when, creating us with an act of inexplicable love, "he imprinted upon us His Face" (Ps 4:6, Vulgate). In creating us in his image, he left imprinted upon us the "record" of his gaze. "He himself has struck our eyes with a fiery ray of His beauty. The measure of the wound already reveals of what sort the arrow is, and the intensity of desire suggests who shot the bolt" (cf. Kabasilas, *Life in Christ*, II; PG 150, 554).

And from that moment our heart is restless; until it finds this gaze again, it thirsts for this face.

For this reason, silently, the Spirit continues to irrigate the parched and arid land of our souls. Like an invisible underground river, like a hidden aquifer, the Spirit does not cease to fertilize the life of men, of all men, speaking to each according to his own language, freshening the salty and bitter waters with which we try to quench our thirst for life and love, and in concealment watering the roots of trees whose fruits and leaves heal our wounds.

But the hidden current of this invisible river rises to the surface of the earth and becomes visible in the Church.

The apostles who were in the Cenacle had all betrayed and abandoned Jesus. They had no merit whatsoever; their desire was their only claim to receive the Spirit. Their whole life was the poverty of waiting and desire. Jesus, in promising them the Spirit, had asked them for nothing else than to "stay": "Stay in the city, until you are clothed with power from on high" (Lk 24:49); "Wait for the promise of the Father" (Acts 1:4). When the Spirit is poured out upon the apostles, upon Mary and the women, the promise of the Father is fulfilled and the Church becomes visible, the Bride of the Lamb descends upon the earth, resplendent with the very glory of God (cf. Rv 21:10–11) because she is poor as God himself is poor, the God-Lamb, who has manifested himself as Servant of the Father and our servant (cf. Jn 13:4).

The thirst of the poor

> When the poor and needy seek water,
>   and there is none,
>   and their tongue is parched with thirst,
> I the LORD will answer them. (Isaiah 41:17)

There are two places where this poverty of the Church shines brightly: the Liturgy and the contemplative life.

In the Liturgy, the Church is shown in all her resplendent and divine poverty, because there she is shown in her deepest reality, as the Bride who receives everything from the Bridegroom. In the Liturgy, the eternal river is poured out without measure and we can drink its water directly from the source.

The other place in which the Church clearly shows her face as the poor Bride is through contemplative life in the desert.

In the desert the Church experiences her poverty, because in the aridity of the desert she has no resources of her own. She is without water and bread. She must rely only on faith in the promise of the Bridegroom: "I am coming soon" (Rv 3:11; 22:7). This spiritual attitude, this desire that the Bridegroom come soon to kiss her because she is lovesick (cf. Song 1:2; 2:5), is the same one whereby Saint Bruno describes his life in the desert. "I live in constant vigilance, waiting for the Lord" (*Letter to Rodolfo*, 4). "I wait, begging that the hand of divine mercy heal all of my weaknesses" (ibid., 3). This "waiting in supplication," this "living in permanent vigilance," this desire that God come to heal us with his Love, with his Spirit, is the heart, the core of life in the desert.

Because, in the end, there is only one thirst that torments us: the thirst to be loved by the Father. There is only one wound that makes our heart bleed: doubt as to being loved. Only the Spirit, only the Love of God in person can heal our wound and quench our thirst, because only the Father loves us truly, without asking for anything in return. The only thing he asks of us in order to quench our thirst with the living water of his Spirit, that is, with the very Love that he has for his only-begotten Son, is that we thirst for him as he thirsts for us (cf. Jn 19:28). The water of life, the Spirit, is given to us according to the measure of our thirst, the extent of our desire, of our poverty. "And let the one who is thirsty come; let the one who desires take *the water of life without price*" (Rv 22:17, emphasis added).

The wait

> How long, O LORD? Will you forget me forever?
>   How long will you hide your face from me?
> (Psalm 13:1)

> Return, my beloved (cf. Song of Songs 2:17) …
> [but] the Bridegroom is delayed. (cf. Matthew 25:5)

Staying, persevering, remaining even though everything seems to say that he will never come, is difficult. But it is this steadfast waiting of the heart that allows the river of living water to flow silently with fullness in us, because:

> The servant who will be loved is the one who stands upright and motionless at the door, in a state of vigil, watchfulness, attentiveness and desire, to open as soon as he hears any knocking.

> Nothing will upset his watchful stillness, not to the slightest degree — neither tiredness, nor hunger, nor entreaties, nor friendly invitations, nor injuries, nor the blows or taunts of his fellows, nor circulation of rumors that his master is dead or displeased with him and intent on harming him. …

"The state of waiting which is rewarded in this way is usually called patience.

"But the Greek word, hypomonē, is infinitely more beautiful and has different associations.

"It signifies a person who waits without moving, in spite of all the blows from those who try to make him move. ...

"They will bring forth fruit with patience." (cf. Lk 8:15) (Simone Weil, *Pensées sans ordre*, in David Rader (ed.), *Gateway to God*, Fontana, London 1974, 71–72)

This "patience" is what allows the river of Living Water to bring forth from our poor soil trees that bear medicinal fruits and leaves. It is this remaining stable that allows him to heal all of our weaknesses, because it lets us experience the gratuitousness of God's love for us. Only if we are truly thirsty can we approach the Heart of God, the spring from which the eternal river of the Spirit flows.

At the Last Supper, Jesus said to the apostles;

Let not your hearts be troubled. Believe in God; believe also in me. In my Father's house are many rooms. If it were not so, would I have told you that I go to prepare a place for you? And if I go and prepare a place for you, I will come again and will take you to myself, that where I am you may be also. (John 14:1–3)

"I will come again and will take you to myself." This

promise of the Lord sustains all of the Church's waiting as long as the present time lasts. A waiting supported by love and hope, but not for this reason any less painful and, at times, difficult.

Of course, "the Church knows that the Lord comes even now in his Eucharist and that he is there in our midst. However, his presence is veiled" (*CCC* 1404).

We have to risk our lives on a reality of which we have no direct experience. Through this faith, we enter into a universe that defies everything the world teaches us. Even the interior consolations, the lights that we receive in prayer, are something transitory and are not God. Moreover, this faith does not belong to us. We cannot obtain it on our own. It is a gift from the Lord that we must ask for and receive with gratitude, while knowing that it will increasingly strip away all of the supports that we still rely on.

We are left with the burning desire to see the Face of the Beloved. This desire entirely fills the prayer of the Psalms: "Hide not your face from me" (Ps 27:9). "When shall I come and appear before God?" (Ps 42:3).

When? And how long?" As Job says, "Behold, I go forward, but he is not there; / and backward, but I do not perceive him; / on the left hand when he is working, I do not behold him; / he turns to the right hand, but I do not see him" (Jb 23:8–9) and yet "even if he should kill me, I would hope in him." (Jb 13:15, Vulgate).

Only the work of the Holy Spirit can bring us to live

in this expectation without wavering, without losing hope. In our hearts, "the Spirit helps us in our weakness. For we do not know what to pray for as we ought, but the Spirit himself intercedes for us with groanings too deep for words" (Rom 8:26). And these "groanings too deep for words" are nothing other than the appeal "Abba-Father" (Rom 8:15; Gal 4:6).

If God leaves us in darkness, and at the same time in the awareness of our sins, it is because he wants us to understand that his goodness is stronger than our evil. Our only future is the infinite mercy of his Heart. This unconditional acceptance offered to us by the "Father of mercies and God of all comfort" (2 Cor 1:3) is what allows us to continue to wait in silence for a healing … that never comes … or at least never comes in the way we expect.

Because in the end our true and final healing is the trusting abandonment of a child in the arms of his mother (cf. Ps 131:2). An abandonment that was the masterpiece of the Holy Spirit in Jesus crucified, when he brought him to cry out his last earthly word:

"Father, into your hands I commit my spirit" (Lk 23:46). It is this abandonment that heals us from discouragement, from the lack of hope. Like Saint Bruno, we continue to "wait in supplication for the hand of divine mercy to heal our inner miseries and satisfy our desire." (*Ad Radulphum*, 3; SC 86, 68)

This filial and pleading abandonment is the cleft that Grace has opened in our hearts of stone and through which the Father will be able to breathe his Spirit into the clay of which we are molded (cf. Gn 2:7) and thus, finally, transform us into his image and likeness (Gn 1:27). In this way the crack will become a wound that will make our heart like that of Jesus, a heart capable of compassion for others and also for ourselves.

Before withdrawing from their sight, the Lord left as an answer to this desire of his Bride, to this expectation of the soul, his last words on earth: "And behold, I am with you always, to the end of the age" (Mt 28:20).

These words are like the viaticum that Jesus wanted to leave to his Church, so that she would not lose heart on the long pilgrimage that, after Easter, she would have to face daily in the darkness of faith.

This promise of the Lord is the only point of support for the Church, which knows and believes that the Risen One has not abandoned her, but accompanies her and supports her day after day with a secret presence that encourages her and nourishes her hope while she waits for the definitive meeting with her spouse, when, as he has promised her, "He will come again and take us with Him" (cf. Jn 14:3).

No longer in figure but in reality the Church, after Easter, relives the experience of the people of Israel, when, after the passage of the Red Sea, God continually accompanied it with his presence during the journey in the desert, but veiled in the pillar of cloud and fire. Now God accompanies the pilgrimage of his people with his presence in the Word and the sacraments, especially in the celebration of the Eucharist; nonetheless, this presence is hidden:

> Hidden in her heart the Church holds a secret and continuous longing, the longing to see again the Face of her Bridegroom, now withdrawn from her eyes. Commenting on verse 82 of Psalm 119, "My eyes fail with watching for thy promise," Saint Ambrose describes this impatient waiting of the Church as that of a "young bride who on a dune on the shore awaits, with tireless anticipation, the arrival of her husband and, with every ship she sees, fancies that her husband is on board, fearing that someone else will have before her the pleasure of seeing her beloved and that she will not be the first to say, 'I saw you!'" (*Expositio in Psalmum 118*, XI, 9; PL 15, 1351)

The silence of God

Often (always?) God's response to this desire for an encounter with him, to this incessant prayer, seems to be his silence.

> On my bed by night
> I sought him whom my soul loves;
>   I sought him, but found him not. (Song of Songs 3:1)

This waiting in the night, this unfulfilled desire for the

Presence to be revealed is the suffering of the Church and of all souls who seek God in prayer.

In fact, even if the Christian is certain of the coming of his Lord, because "it is impossible for God to lie" (Heb 6:18), God's silence seems to be the only answer to our desire to see him, a response that only makes the desire grow and increase. But this watchful waiting in the night, the dark and painful waiting that the Church lives, this waiting that seems never to end, helps us to understand and share from within the experience lived today by so much of humanity, our brothers. Disillusioned, they live a meaningless life, and yet they continue to wish, often unconsciously, that something would happen, that something, or someone, would finally come to give meaning to their existence, to free them from the emptiness.

> The terrible mystery of Holy Saturday, its abyss of silence, has thus acquired a crushing reality in these days of ours. For, this is Holy Saturday: the day of God's concealment. … Holy Saturday: the day God was buried; is not this the day we are living now, and formidably so? Did not our century mark the start of one long Holy Saturday, the day God was absent …? The divine darkness of this day, of this century which is increasingly becoming one long Holy Saturday, is speaking to our conscience. It is one of our concerns. (J Ratzinger, *Ser Cristiano*, Salamanca 1967, 88–89)

God is silent and this silence pierces the soul of the person praying, who ceaselessly calls but receives no answer. Day and night succeed one another in an unflagging quest for a word, for help that does not come, God seems so distant, so forgetful, so absent. The prayer asks to be heard, to be answered, it begs for contact, seeks a relationship that can give comfort and salvation. But if God fails to respond, the cry of help is lost in the void and loneliness becomes unbearable." (Benedict XVI, general audience, September 14, 2011)

Saint Bruno saw his life in solitude as a persevering wait, watching like a sentry in the night for the arrival of the Bridegroom, to open for him right away (*Ad Radulphum*, 4; SC 86, 68). St. John of the Cross, in his *Spiritual Canticle*, has wonderful verses to describe this waiting and desire of the Bride:

Where have You hidden Yourself,
Beloved, and left me in my groaning?
Like the deer You have fled,
having wounded me.
I set out after You, calling aloud; but You had gone.
(*Spiritual Canticle* B, 1)

But as long as time lasts, we will be given no other presence of Christ than that which faith gives us. The Church knows this, and yet, until the end of time, the Spirit and the Bride, tirelessly, beseech the Lord: "Come!" (cf. Rv 22:17).

But the wait is long and the Bridegroom is late in coming (cf. Mt 25:5). Often the Lord even seems to be sleeping (Mk 4:38) and to have forgotten his Bride, so much so that the little bark of the Church, which is trying to cross the sea by night (Jn 6:16–17) to get to "the other side" (Mk 4:35), sometimes seems to be sinking amid the storm (Mt 8:24).

But this painful experience of the absence and silence of God that the Church experiences is not something "anomalous," nor should it surprise us. It is nothing other than the participation, in the flow of time, of what her Lord himself experienced when, "in the days of his flesh, Jesus offered up prayers and supplications, with loud cries and tears, to him who was able to save him from death" (Heb 5:7). This experience of the concealment of God is nothing other than the continuation, in the Church, of the Lord's Paschal mystery.

With him, in him and through him, through the darkness of the cross and the sepulchre, the Church is passing from this world to the Father, from slavery to freedom, from death to life. And the Passover, as we know, happened "at night."

This longing for Christ, this desire to see him again, this painful waiting in the night, is something that the Church lives in a particularly intense way in the monks, in those who have been called by Christ to be in a special way living and transparent signs of his Paschal mystery for his whole Mystical Body.

They are those who have been called to live as sentinels, who peer into the night for the first signs of the dawn: "Watchman, what time of the night?" (Is 21:11).

The longing and desire to "see Christ," to "see the Face of the Lord" (cf. Ps 27 (26), 8), they are the indelible mark that the Fire of the Spirit has imprinted in the hearts of all who seek God, in the heart of each of us, called by him to live the mystery of "persevering divine vigilance, awaiting His return, to open for Him immediately as soon as He knocks" (Saint Bruno, *Ad Radulphum,* 4; SC 86, 68).

Yet sometimes all this seems like an illusion, and we seem to find ourselves with empty hands, or worse, to be holding in our hands only the rubble of the life we had dreamed of. When everything seems to crumble in us and around us, when our weakness and sin seem to be a burden that we will never be able to shake off, when the hidden ghosts that we bear in the secret recesses of the heart are violently exposed, when failure seems like the only horizon open before us — how many times do we ask ourselves, in the silence of our heart, if this waiting for the Lord will ever be over, or whether it is just an illusion and perhaps we must admit that we were wrong? How many times have we waited "for peace, / but no good came" (cf. Jer 14:19)? We have done our best to accomplish the Will of God, to be faithful to him. We have watched long in order to be ready to welcome him right away, as soon as he knocked, even faintly, and instead, not only has he not come, but it seems he has gone even farther away.

But this means forgetting:

That the Father's love has penetrated our lives through the wounded Heart of Christ, thus suggesting that perhaps it is only through the pierced heart that the Father enters into every human life: the heart broken by the pain of sins, evils, failures, the 'mess' to which it has reduced the gift of life, by the absurdity and degradation to which it has reduced itself. (John Navone, SJ, *Teologia del Fallimento*, Edizioni Paoline, 1976, 12)

How else but through a broken heart
May Lord Christ enter in?
(Oscar Wilde, *The Ballad of Reading Gaol*, V, 83–84)

This persevering in waiting, this wearing out of the eyes amid the darkness of the night while peering for the arrival of the Word (cf. Ps 119:82), this stubborn hope in the coming of God, although everything appears to say the opposite, in reality is the only way we have to tell the Father, with poverty but with truth, of our desire for communion with him. This is the only thing he asks of us. The Father cannot resist this desire that in spite of everything obstinately perseveres in waiting for him. Because this desire is the work of the Spirit of Christ in us.

In the bitter cold of this night, when all seems lost, it is there that the song of praise reaches its greatest purity.

Paradoxically, it is from the depths of this underworld, *de ventre inferi* (Jon 2:3) that the purest hymn rises to the Father: "No one sings so purely as those who are in the deepest hell; what we believe to be the song of angels is their song" (Franz Kafka, *Lettere a Milena*, Milan 1988, 186).

The purification of hope

"The Lord brought them out, set them free, in hope" (cf. Ps 78:53): in fact, it is only in hope that the Church, and we in it, live this intimacy with the Father, the fruit of Christ's Passover; it is in hope that we now participate in his Paschal mystery, in his "passage." But, even if lived only in hope, this intimacy is already real.

However dark may be the path down which the Lord leads his Church, and us in it; however incomprehensible what we experience on a daily basis; however seemingly devoid of light the future that awaits us, we are sure that we are in the hands of the Father and that he is leading us towards the fullness of the Paschal mystery. It is towards the Promised Land of intimacy with him who is guiding us through our desert, because, as he has told us. "For I know the plans I have for you … plans for welfare and not for evil, to give you a future and a hope. Then you will call upon me and come and pray to me, and I will hear you. You will seek me and find me; when you seek me with all your heart. I will be found by you" (Jer 29:11–14). "And behold, I am with you always, to the end of the age" (Mt 28:20). But, "I am with you in silence." "I speak to you with 'a voice of silence'" (cf. 1 Kgs 19:12).

> The silence of God can be mistaken for the absence or death of God, if one thinks that only the word is an indication of care and existence. But in the case of God the fullness of love, the anticipation that man may be freed from the prison of the finite and of idols, expresses itself through that silence which is not non-existence or incommunicability, but rather word beyond words, Word without words. (Karl Rahner, SF, cited in *L'Osservatore Romano* 70, 26 March 2005, 12)

In fact, beyond what we can "experience," beyond sentiments and emotions, beyond our subjective state, there is a "place," hidden in the depths of our heart, where we are immediately "touched" by him, where we are in communion with him through faith, hope and love. This divine "touch" happens "in silence" because it is God who is begetting God in us: "My Father will love him, and we will come to him and make our home with him" (Jn 14:23). This is beyond and above every possible word. In fact, "in this silence, unbearable to the 'outer' man, the Father speaks to us his incarnate Word, who suffered, died, and rose; in this silence the Spirit of adoption enables us to share in the prayer of Jesus" (*CCC* 2717).

This silence as God's only response to our prayer is what allows us to purify our image of God, and thus to be able to escape the temptation to turn prayer into a "trade" between equals. As it was for Job, who, at the end of his struggle with God, faced with the splendor of the mystery of God, had to recognize that "I had heard of you by the hearing of the ear, / but now my eye sees you" (Job 42:5), this silence, this "absence" of God is the necessary purification of all those who pray, so that they may attain to the "vision" of the true God:

> Faith certainly contains the elements of firmness, of absolute trust, of self-surrender, but also the element of darkness. ... The category of 'cooperation' that is so dear to us breaks down in reference to God, because it does not allow sufficient expression of God's sublimity and the hidden nature of His activity. And indeed it is only the man who has opened himself unreservedly to God who comes to accept the otherness of God, the obscurity of His Will, which can turn into a sword that passes through our own. (cf. Lk 2:35) (Joseph Ratzinger, "Llena eres de Gracia," in Ratzinger, Balthasar, *María, Iglesia Naciente*, Madrid 1999, 52)

This experience of God's silence, of the apparent "failure" of prayer, is absolutely necessary. In fact, all of us, individuals and the Church, are always exposed to the subtle worldly temptation of utopia, the belief that salvation can be achieved in history, in our personal history and in that of the Church. More or less consciously, we are convinced that the Kingdom will be born from the irrepressible spiritual perfection of the individual and the community. That the "magnificent and progressive fates" are unstoppable and are the sure path by which the Kingdom will arrive among us. On the contrary, as the *Catechism* teaches:

> The kingdom will be fulfilled, then, not by a historic triumph of the Church through a progressive ascendancy, but only by God's victory over the final unleashing of evil, which will cause his Bride to come down from heaven (cf. Rv 13:8; 20:7–10; 21:2–4). (677)

God's silence "obliges" us to recall that "without Him we can do *nothing*" (cf. Jn 15:5). "Nothing." Perhaps we do not fully realize that "nothing" means "nothing" … not "little." It is necessary that the body and all the individual members experience and live within themselves the radical weakness of the crucified Head, nailed down and powerless. Because it was only when, in Christ, poverty came to this insurmountable abyss, it was only then that in human terms he could say to the full, "Abba, Father." And only when each of us, in the measure established by the Father, really communes with this poverty of Christ, it is only then that each of us, and therefore the whole Church, will be fully what the Father had planned for us from eternity.

It is perhaps in this light that we should interpret the humiliating trials that the Church is experiencing and going through in our time, because "before Christ's second coming the Church must pass through a final trial that will shake the faith of many believers (cf. Lk 18:8; Mt 24:12)" (*CCC* 675).

It is a good thing that the ministry should experience today this denigrated face, that Judas should betray it once again, in every sense. ... The more visibly the Head covered with blood and wounds shines through the face of the ministry, the more pure the ministerial existence will be within itself. (Hans Urs von Balthasar, *María Iglesia Naciente*, 138–139)

If on the one hand the current grave crisis that the Church is experiencing is a liberation from the temptation of the utopian possibility of an infra-historical and intra-worldly realisation of the Kingdom, on the other hand the current sufferings are "the pains of childbirth" (cf. Rv 12:2) in which the Church is bringing Christ forth in the world.

Because the Church can be understood only in relation to her Lord. There is no self-comprehension of the Church. She will always allow the Lord to give her meaning, and will welcome this revelation of herself with humble love: He has looked upon the lowliness of His handmaiden. (von Balthasar, *María Iglesia Naciente*, 139)

And this gift of herself that she receives from the Lord never fails. The faithfulness of Christ to his Bride, to every soul, is indefectible. For this reason, "despite the hostility of the Dragon, the Church *always* brings Christ forth" (Bede, *Explanatio Apocalypsis*, II, 12; PL 93, 166; emphasis added). And thus, in poverty welcoming the gift of herself from Christ, with him and through him, the Church "every day brings herself forth" (Bede, *Explanatio*, *op. cit.* ibid.).

The Desert

_____

The church of the desert (cf. Acts 7:38)

There is a "place" where this waiting for God in silence and poverty of spirit is fulfilled. There is a "place" where the encounter between the Bridegroom and the Bride, an encounter that is the eternal desire of God and the restlessness of the human heart, comes about. In this "place" God reveals, in faith, his true face to those who are longing for it in the humiliation of their incurable poverty. This place is the desert.

The desert is, etymologically, an "abandoned place," a place from which all have fled because it lacks the necessities of life. This is why there is solitude in the desert. No one goes to the desert; indeed, the desert is such because everyone has abandoned it.

The desert, in fact, is a place where the human being experiences his vulnerability and finds himself in complete powerlessness, without the usual supports, so that he has to admit and face his own mortality. The desert is the sign of our complete powerlessness because it is there that our weakness is revealed, because one cannot survive in the desert. In it there is a lack of bread and water, a lack of the normal relationships with others that allow us to live. In the desert man discovers himself in his truth: "wretched, pitiable, poor, blind, and naked" (Rv 3:17). This is why the desert is a place where no one wants to go, much less stay. No one can go into the desert on his own initiative. Only the Spirit can sound the call to the desert, as he did with Christ (cf. Mt 4:1; Lk 4:1–2); Saint Mark even says that the Spirit "drove him out" into the desert (Mk 1:12).

For this reason, as the Lord himself states, it is he who leads his Bride to the desert: "I will allure her, / and bring her into the wilderness, / and speak tenderly to her" (Hos 2:14). It is there, in solitude, that God has prepared a refuge for the Woman, to "speak tenderly to her," to nourish her (cf. Rv 12:6) with his Word. It is there that destruction will finally come to the deformed image of God in us that we had received as an inheritance from our first father, and we will receive from God the revelation of his true face: that of a Bridegroom in love, and not of a despot. There "you will call me 'My Husband,' and no longer will you call me 'My Baal'" (Hos 2:16). It is only through being stripped bare in the desert that "one acquires that serene gaze which wounds the Bridegroom with love, and through whose transparency and purity one sees God" (Saint Bruno, *Ad Radulphum* 6; SC 86, 70).

Like the Church, each of us is "drawn" by the Spirit

into the desert. He brings us the insight that in the desert there is something, Someone, that makes it alluring. And this attraction is stronger than the instinctive fear of the desert. "What makes the desert beautiful," says the Little Prince, "is that somewhere it hides a well" (A. de Saint-Exupéry, *Le Petit Prince*, Paris 2007, 82). It is true; hidden in the depths of the desert there is a well, and on the edge of this well Jesus is seated, alone, waiting for us, to say to us, "Give me a drink" (Jn 4:7). And this woman of whom Jesus asks a drink "is a figure of the Church" (Saint Augustine, *In Joannis Evangelium*, XV, 10; PL 35, 1313).

If in the desert man experiences thirst, to the point of death, in the desert we meet Jesus, who reveals to us that God too has a thirst, and a thirst for us that will lead him to death, to the cross, where he will die of thirst (cf. Jn 19:28). This revelation of God's thirst will be the fulfillment of all the Scriptures (ibid.).

There is therefore a desert even for God, and this desert is the absence of man, the refusal of man who does not want to reciprocate his divine love.

But God persists in his desire to find someone who truly reciprocates his love (cf. Jn 4:23), so he seduces the Church, lures her into the desert to speak to her heart (Hos 2:14). Only in the desert, when all sounds and voices fall silent, only then can God speak to our hearts and show us his true face. Not that of an almighty Pharaoh, but that of a lover, thirsty for the love of his bride.

In fact it is only here, by the sheer force of the desert stripped bare of the flimsy supports that constituted our fragile security and gave us the illusion of a "good" life, that we come face to face with "our demons" and with "the wild beasts that we have nourished in our hearts from time immemorial" (Guigo II, *Meditatio* I; SC 163, 126–127). Here our wickedness, our vices and our perverse inclinations come out into the light of day, without our being able to hide them. In the desert we are stripped of everything. In the desert our pride, especially spiritual pride, is reduced to silence.

Thus, only when the din of the prideful effort that we continually make to save ourselves by our own strength is extinguished within us, only then, in the silence of the desert, will we be able to hear the whisper of God, who speaks "with a gentle breeze, with the voice of silence" (cf. 1 Kgs 19:12). Only then, in fact, will God be able to speak to our hearts and tell us how incomprehensible and great is his love for each of us. Only when in solitude we have the humiliating experience of our incurable misery, only then will we be able to truly "see" the true Face of God. And then we will truly realise that the only reason God has led us into the wilderness is "for his mercy endures for ever" (cf. Ps 136). He led us into solitude so that we could have the concrete experience that in the desert man "awaits everything from the mercy of God and nothing from his own merits" (Guigo, *Letter on the Solitary Life*, 4; SC 86, 142).

Only if we allow ourselves to be led by the Spirit "*ad*

interiora deserti" (Ex 3:1, Vulgate), to the "inner parts of the desert," will we be able to discover the Burning Bush from which God has always called us, individuals and the Church. And there, prostrate in silence, barefoot and with covered face, we will be able to receive the revelation of his name.

And it is only in the Paschal mystery, that is, in the revelation that he makes of himself in the burning bush of the cross and Resurrection of his Son, where Christ burns without being consumed in the fire of the Spirit, in the fire of love for the Father and for us, it is only there that we can "see" God in his truth.

But Christ's Passover took place in the deepest solitude and in the most total silence: who can say, in fact, at what moment Christ rose?

"O truly blessed night," sings the "Exultet" of Easter, "worthy alone to know the time and hour when Christ rose from the underworld!"

For this reason the desert is the setting of the most perfect celebration of Easter (cf. Eucherius of Lyon, *Epistola de Laude Eremi* 32; PL 50, 708), and "truly the Cross of Christ is called hermitage, and true hermit is Christ God who carries the Cross" (Anonymous 13th century text cited by J Leclercq in *Archives d'histoire Doctrinale et Littéraire du Moyen Âge,* 31, 1964, 41).

Thus it is only in the solitude and silence of an Easter night that the Church, and we in it and with it, will be able to fully and definitively experience our complete communion with the death and resurrection of

Christ, our Pascha. "The Church will enter the glory of the kingdom only through this final Passover, when she will follow her Lord in his death and Resurrection (cf. Rv 19:1–9)" (*CCC* 677). And in the nocturnal silence of this Passover of ours there will be revealed to us, in the Face of the crucified and risen Son, the true Face of the Father.

Ultimately, the whole life of prayer is summed up in and focused on allowing Christ to live in us his life of praise and offering to the Father. Everything converges in living his Paschal mystery with him. In sharing, in the luminous obscurity of faith now, and after death in the dazzling light of the Resurrection, the profound silence and immense solitude of his "Easter night."

The Risen Life

"I am my beloved's and my beloved is mine"
(Song 6:3)

Everything said so far may perhaps seem very "intimistic," even "alienating," far from the so often tragic reality of our world and our Church.

It all seems like a fairy tale, yet this is our faith, and to bear witness to this truth with our lives is the only reason that Christians and the Church have to exist.

All of this can seem like a fable only if one forgets that the Paschal mystery is the *only* event that has definitively and radically changed history. As cited above, it is:

> The unique event of history which does not pass away. … His Paschal mystery is a real event that occurred in our history, but it is unique: all other historical events happen once, and then they pass away, swallowed up in the past. The Paschal mystery of Christ, by contrast, cannot remain only in the past, because by his death he

destroyed death. … The event of the Cross and Resurrection abides and draws everything toward life. (*CCC* 1085)

This contemporaneity of Easter with all moments of all times is the reason why every man can have a *real* experience of Easter, of the real presence of the Risen One in his own life.

And it is this contemporaneity of the Risen One with all men of all times that allows our prayer not to be a self-delusion, an empty reverie, or, worse, a delirium in which we are speaking to ourselves or to the void.

It is therefore above all in prayer that the Risen Christ, alive and present, present and active, "here and now" continues to draw all men to himself (cf. Jn 12:32), drawing them into his mystery.

Saint Bruno, in his letter to Rodolfo, left us a sober but compelling description of his experience of this intervention of the Risen One in his life, an experience that gave new direction to his existence.

One day when we were together, you and I and One-Eyed Folco, in the little garden next to Adam's house, where I was staying at the time, we talked for a little while, it seems to me, of the false pleasures and perishing riches of this world, and also of the joys of eternal glory. Then, aflame with divine love, we promised, we made a vow and we decided to leave the fleeting realities of the world behind as soon as possible and take hold of what is eternal. (Saint Bruno, *Ad Radulphum* 13; SC 86, 74–76)

Prayer is therefore the "door" that allows Christ to truly enter into our lives, to lure us into the desert and speak to our hearts (cf. Hos 2:14). Prayer, even the poorest, is the only "door" through which the Risen One can burst through into us and into our world (Rv 4:1). And his bursting through always surprises us … because he, in the sovereign freedom of his love, claims the right to "surprise" even those who may not expect him or expect him unconsciously.

Keeping close to our time and close to the restlessness of our modern age, how can we fail to recall the conversion of Simone Weil? This is how she recounts it in *Waiting for God*. It was while reciting a poem by George Herbert:

I thought I was reciting it only as a beautiful poem (the poem 'Love' by the English poet George Herbert, d. 1633), but unbeknownst to me that recitation had the virtue of a prayer. It was just as I was reciting it that Christ came down and took hold of me. In my reasoning on the insolubility of the problem of God I had not foreseen this possibility of real contact, person-to-person, down here, between a human being and God.

Then again, neither the senses nor the imagination had played the slightest part in this sudden conquest of Christ; I only felt, through suffering, the presence of a love similar to that which can be discerned in the smile of a beloved face. (Simone Weil, *Attente de Dieu*, Paris 1966, 75–76)

In fact, prayer, even the most tiresome, the driest, the most distracted, that which seems to fall always and inexorably into the void, is always heard, because its hearer is always alive and present. It is always "real contact, person to person, down here, between a human being and God."

Therefore, a Church that prays, a Christian who prays, allowing Christ to really draw them, burst into their lives and continue to live his Paschal mystery in them, are supremely "efficacious" because they make present, albeit amid immense poverty and limitation, the only originality that exists in our universe, the only event that truly matters: the gift of God's very Life to us men. And, for this very reason, the destruction of death.

"Love is strong as death" (Song 8:6)

Because death, our death, however much it may be exorcised, silenced, hidden, remains the only true problem for each of us.

Those who believe in the Risen One may not realize that for a nonbeliever:

It is life itself that is struck down by death. Because he 'knows' that everything that is important and valuable to him in the present is sentenced to death in the future. Whatever he may love, he loves what must die. Life turns into the realization of death. Everything is invaded by nothingness and the absurd. (Madeleine Dêlbrel, *Nous Autres, Gens des Rues*, Paris 1966, 208–209)

Everything man does is an attempt to escape the anguish of *his* death which he *knows* will come, in spite of everything:

[The] words of the Risen Christ to the Father have also become words which the Lord speaks to us: 'I arose and now I am still with you,' he says to each of us. "My hand upholds you. Wherever you may fall, you will always fall into my hands. I am present even at the door of death. Where no one can accompany you further, and where you can bring nothing, even there I am waiting for you, and for you I will change darkness into light." (Benedict XVI, Easter Vigil homily, April 7, 2007)

In fact:

If God's coming as man had not reached this depth, God would have been mocking him. In becoming man, God heads towards the bosom of death, enters it, and this is the decisive event, the unique event. Jesus, the victor over death with His death, who gives us His Life: this is the unique Event of history, His Cross and His Resurrection. (J Corbon, *Liturgia alla Sorgente*, Bose, 2003, 40–41)

And this event becomes "ours" daily in prayer. Because prayer either is communion with the Risen One or it is not. He who prays, uniting himself with Jesus in faith, "*has* eternal life. He does not come into judgment, but has passed from death to life," as the Lord himself states (Jn 5:24, emphasis added).

When he prays, the Christian "*has* eternal life": he already possesses it. He has *already* passed with Christ from death to life, because he welcomes into himself Christ *alive*, and alive *today*, alive in the unique Act that gives him life, receiving life from the Father and returning it in the Eucharist. With prayer we pass from a life that is bound for death and has death as its only horizon to the endless Life that springs from the gift of self to the utmost, unto death.

For those who pray, Christ's Paschal mystery has become their own life, so much so that they can say, "It is no longer I who live, but Christ who lives in me" (Gal 2:20). For a Christian there is nothing that can be foreign to the new life, to the Paschal life of Christ with which he is in intimate contact through prayer, through the sacraments of the Liturgy.

For this reason Paul can ask the baptized, "*Whatev-*

er you do, in word or deed, do everything in the name of the Lord Jesus, giving thanks to God the Father through him." (Col 3:17, emphasis added). "Whatever," namely "everything." In every action, in every word, in every activity, in every moment lived with love, in obedience to the will of God, we "pass" with Christ to the Father, and in this "passing," in this "passage" we draw with us everyone and everything. Because the power of the Paschal mystery envelops and transforms everything. And so everything can really become prayer.

Our every word, our every action, even, and perhaps above all, the smallest and most trivial, the most natural, such as sleeping and eating, breathing and walking, what we do out of habit or for necessity, these can become an echo of Jesus's "yes" to the Father, if with a gaze of faith we recognize in them the Father's invitation to carry out his will.

Throughout our day, often so "normal," so "trivial," we can find an infinity of moments in which to say to the Father with Jesus,

> Sacrifices and offerings you have not desired,
>   but a body have you prepared for me …
> Then I said, "Behold, I have come to do your will,
>   O God." (Hebrews 10:5–7)

Because all the little everyday things are the "material," "the body" that God offers us so that our love for him may not remain a word, an empty sentiment, but instead take a "body."

In this way our whole person, in all its dimensions, will be able to become truly and concretely a prolongation of the Incarnation, an "additional humanity in which [Christ] may renew all His Mystery" (St. Elizabeth of the Trinity, *Elevazione alla Santissima Trinità*). Thus our person will become Church.

The Mother of Prayer

―――――

**"I came to my garden, my sister, my bride"
(Song 5:1)**
In the poor history of our world, one day such a complete and total "yes" was spoken that it allowed God to really become embodied in our universe. There was a "yes" without reservations, issued from a heart so clear and without self-seeking that it really drew God to the earth.

Mary.

There was a day when God knocked on the door of a little village house, knocked on the door of a maiden of no renown, asking her, "Open to me, my sister, my love, / my dove, my perfect one" (Song 5:2). And she opened for him right away. So "the Word became flesh and dwelt among us" (Jn 1:14).

Through Mary's silent faith, the praise that the Word eternally sings to the Father — "Abba" — he began to sing this in our world too, with our own words. Prayer became flesh, became visible and tangible, so that all of us could sing with the Son his eternal song to the Father. Because it was that "yes" of the Virgin which finally allowed "humanity to loosen its mute tongue in holy and sincere prayers and feel that ineffable regenerating force of the spirit which is inherent in singing the praises of God, through Jesus Christ and in the Holy Spirit" (St. Paul VI, speech, December 4, 1963, 11).

And the first to join in this song was the Virgin herself, with her *Magnificat*.

A song that the Church has made its own and sings daily at the setting of the sun, making its own the call of Saint Ambrose: "Let the soul of Mary be in each one to magnify the Lord, and in each one the spirit of Mary to rejoice in God" (*In Lucam*, 2, 26; PL 15, 1561). So that she, Mary, is ever *tympanistria nostra* (Saint Augustine, *Attributed Sermons*, sermon 194, 2; PL 39, 2105) who still today leads the thanksgiving song of the Church, leads the choir of the voices of the faithful who in prayer praise God for the salvation he has wrought in them.

"Mary treasured up all these things, pondering them in her heart" (Lk 2:19). Memory first, awareness next, then understanding, wonder, contemplation; in the end, are not perhaps the phases of Our Lady's spiritual life raised up, also in this respect, as the example, as the type of the internal process that should take place in every follower of Christ?

Jesus is present, first of all, through faith, within us: 'That Christ may dwell in your hearts through faith' (Eph 3:17). From this statement (which will then be completed with another essential element, Grace, and another instrumental coefficient, the Church), stems the whole spiritual life of our religion." (St. Paul VI, general audience, September 1, 1974)

In the Gospel of Luke, Jesus says, "My mother and my brothers are those who hear the word of God and do it" (Lk 8:21). And Saint Ambrose comments, "Every soul that believes conceives and begets the Word of God … If there is only one Mother of Christ according to the flesh, according to the faith Christ is begotten of all" (Saint Ambrose, *op. cit.*). Mary is therefore the Mother of prayer, of us and of the Church, because she is the mother of the one who knows and makes prayer. To the extent of our faith, always, silently, Mary is begetting Christ in us and with us, and for this very reason she is begetting our prayer.

And above all she begets the prayer of the poor, of those who "do not know what to pray as [they] ought" (Rom 8:26), who do not know and cannot travel the arduous ways of "great" prayer. To these "little souls" God offers Mary as a simple path of prayer, as an easy means for their transformation in Christ:

"May this great Mother be forever praised, full of Majesty, at whose knee I learned everything." Yes, may this Mother be forever praised, at whose knee we learned everything, and where every day we continue to learn everything. (P. Claudel, quoted by H. de Lubac, *Meditación sobre la Iglesia*, Madrid 2008, 295)

Yes, with Mary we are like little children babbling their first prayers at the knee of the mother who teaches them to them.

For this reason, St. Louis Marie Grignon de Montfort wrote in his *A Treatise on the True Devotion to the Blessed Virgin*:

There is a great difference between making a figure in relief by blows of hammer and chisel, and making a figure by throwing it into a mold. Statuaries and sculptors labor much to make figures in the first manner; but to make them in the second manner, they work little, and do their work quickly.

Saint Augustine calls our Blessed Lady *forma Dei*, 'the mold of God' ... 'the mold fit to cast and mold gods.' He who is cast in this mold is presently formed and molded in Jesus Christ, and Jesus Christ in him. At a slight expense and in a short time he will become God, because he has been cast in the same mold which has formed a God. ...

Without trusting to their own skill, but only in the goodness of the mold, they cast themselves and lose themselves in Mary, to become the portraits of Jesus Christ after nature. …

But remember that we only cast in a mold what is melted and liquid; that is to say, you must destroy and melt down in yourself the old Adam to become the new one in Mary. (Louis-Marie Grignion de Montfort, Frederick William Faber (tr.), *A Treatise on the True Devotion to the Blessed Virgin*, Burns and Lambert, London 1863, 156–157)

And when, by the work of the Holy Spirit and the prayer of Mary, Christ has been perfectly formed in all, when he has reached his full stature, then his song will be sung perfectly by his Body, by his Church. Then the new Jerusalem will come down from heaven shining with the glory of God, and will no longer need any place of prayer, any temple, because God himself and Christ will be its temple. Then, in fact, the communion of the Holy Trinity, the eternal song that the Son sings to the Father in the Holy Spirit, will spread incessantly and fully in all the glorified members of the Risen One (cf. J. Corbon, *Liturgia alla Sorgente, op. cit.*, 52):

Then the Church will go to the place of her kingdom, having with her only her spiritual members, disjoined and separated forever from all that is impure: a truly holy city, truly triumphant, the kingdom of Jesus Christ, and reigning with Jesus Christ.

While waiting for that day, she moans down

here like an exile: seated, as the holy Psalmist says, by the streams of Babylon, weeping and moaning, remembering Zion: Seated by the streams, stable amid the changes; not carried off by the streams, but sighing on their banks; seeing that all things flow away, and sighing for Zion, where all things are permanent; weeping to be in the midst of that which passes and is not, for the memory she has in her heart of what endures and is: such are the moans of this exile.

Meanwhile she sings for consolation, and sings the same song of the heavenly Jerusalem: Alleluia, God be praised; Amen, so be it! Praise be to God for His great glory; this is the song of the Church. This part of her, which is already alive with God, sings it to the full, and the other, in faithful echo, repeats it in the impatience and greed of a holy desire.

Alleluia for the Church, praise God for the Church: praise God when He knocks, praise God when He gives: Amen, so be it for the Church that continually says, He has done all things well! (J B Bossuet, *Lettre (IV) à une Demoiselle de Metz*, nos. 20–22)

Conclusion

———

We are aware that the previous notes, rather than dealing comprehensively with the topic proposed to us, have only touched upon it. However, since, as St. Paul VI said, "Modern man listens more willingly to witnesses than to teachers, and if he does listen to teachers, it is because they are witnesses" (*Evangelii Nuntiandi*, 41), we conclude these few reflections with the lived testimony of prayer of a monk who has spent his long life in this incessant search for the Face of God.

Prayer, Experience of God

————

Prayer for the Carthusian monk

The classic definition of prayer is that of John Damascene, "a raising of the soul to God" (cf. *CCC* 2559). However, the Carthusian will perhaps prefer the definition of the monk John Climacus, who calls prayer "converse" with God (*Ladder*, step 28. He also adds that prayer is union with God, *enôsis*!). We use the word "converse" to translate *homilia*, a word that designates habitual contact with someone — a being-with.

In the Carthusian Order, Guigo, the author of the first rule (actually a simple collection of customs) writes, almost in passing (this is his style), a key sentence: "Our main application and our vocation are to live in the silence and solitude of the cell" (*Consuetudines Cartusiae*, 14, 5). Nonetheless, we must remember what William of Saint-Thierry, a Cistercian monk who was a great friend of the Carthusians, said: "The monk is never less alone than when he is alone," because in solitude the monk is with God. So for him prayer will be nothing other than living this situation.

Carthusian founder Saint Bruno, in one of the few letters we have from him, wrote: "What benefit and divine joy the solitude and silence of the desert bring to those who love them, only those who have experienced them know" (*Ad Radulphum,* 6). It is therefore a matter of "experience." But we must say right away that this "experience" can be lived in complete darkness, in the absence of any sentiment. This is very difficult for the man of today to understand: yet understanding it is the precious pearl hidden in the Carthusian vocation.

At the level of what is perceived, of what the monk experiences quite often, there may be simply the fact that he "endures," that in spite of everything he continues to live in solitude. Despite the trials, despite at times the temptation to run away, he perseveres, because the depth of his heart cleaves to this way of life. Because in this constancy God is present. It is he, and he alone, who gives us the strength to persevere.

Bruno himself teaches this in another letter to the Brothers of Chartreuse. Many, he said, have desired this solitude, but could not remain there, "because they did not receive the grace of it from above — *Nulli eorum desuper concessum est.*"

Although today some prefer to talk about the psychological causes of vocation or lack of vocation, this observation by Saint Bruno is fundamental. The reality is this: we can remain in solitude because we are upheld by God. The human factors, what we feel, whether positive or negative, certainly exist; but after long experience we realize that these factors do not reach the profound reality that is within us. It is beyond the level of feeling.

And the profound reality is that I know by faith that God is there, in me, and he is the one who carries me. I know it in faith. Faith is not just a cry, it is knowledge. Because there are many different forms of human knowledge or understanding. But at the summit is "superknowledge" (*epignôsis*): this is a neologism coined by Saint Paul to describe the light that God puts within us (cf. Eph 4:13). The understanding of faith is a divine light secretly present in my spirit, which allows me to see by this received light and no other means that "all this is true," and first of all precisely that God is there in me. I cannot "lay claim" to this light to scrutinize it, but it is in me.

This quick sketch of what faith is has not diverted us from the topic of prayer. Prayer is a "converse" with God because it consists in living a reality that has already been given to me, that is, the God who is present, here, in my very faith.

What does it mean to live this? Faith, because it is a divine Presence within me, "touches" God in the darkness. He who wants to live by this will not be able to content himself with the representations of God that he has in his mind, nor the little emotional movements he has in his heart. Eckhart, in his little treatise "On instruction," writes these crucial words: "What we seek is not the God who presents himself to our mind in the form of thoughts and feelings, because when these thoughts and feelings disappear, that God also disappears. What we want is the very Reality of God, well beyond every thought and sentiment."

How can this be achieved? The Carthusian Statutes say that the path of the monk consists in being "introduced by the Holy Spirit into the depths of his heart" (4, 2). Here is the echo of a very profound conviction, which has been present in all solitary monks. Solitary monks are certain that they carry deep within themselves an abyss of Light. Most of the time, this Light remains completely hidden from them. But this hardly matters. This abyss of Light draws them; it is the true source of that "divine joy" of which Saint Bruno spoke.

Only the Holy Spirit can move us in this direction. We need do nothing else, therefore, than let God himself act in us. In his prayer, the monk is totally receptive.

Praying means letting God act. One consequence of this is that the monk is called to a total self-despoilment. Because authentic receptivity, if it is not just a pious desire, requires a long and hard apprenticeship. Mother Teresa of Calcutta said, "Love hurts" (that is, it hurts the one who loves, obviously).

It is not up to us to tell the Lord when to act. The monk fundamentally lives in a state of waiting: waiting for the day when his Lord will come (cf. Lk 12:26), that is, when the Lord will fully manifest himself as he is.

"Blessed is the soul who, awaiting the arrival of her Lord this very day, considers as nothing all the fatigue of the day and the fatigue of the night, because she knows that at the first light of dawn her Lord will manifest himself" (PG 90, 1401). Thus spoke the monk Elias Ekdikos, a near-contemporary of Saint Bruno, who had shared exactly the same thought (cf. *Ad Radulphum*, 4).

But there is another aspect of prayer. Here our humanity regains its rights. For to assimilate, as a human being, this divine reality that is within me, I must also exercise my faculties: intelligence, will, sentiment. John van Ruysbroeck, whose writings have been the favorite reading of many Carthusians in past centuries, explains:

> Grace flows from God himself as an interior move-ment, an influence of the Holy Spirit who acts on our spirit from within, not from without. Because God is more intimate to us than we are ourselves, and His movement is closer to us than our own action. Thus God works in us from the inside out, while created things work in us from the outside in. (*Ornamento Nozze Spirituali* 1, 55)

To pray, therefore, simply means allowing God to act within me. In order that God may act, a certain amount of prayer activity may be necessary, for example for some people the prolonged recitation of the Rosary, etc. But this activity has value only because God prays in me through it. Saint Paul said that no one can say "Jesus is Lord" unless he is moved by the Holy Spirit (cf. 1 Cor 12:3). This is even more true of all the concrete forms of prayer that the monk can use. In all cases, what really matters is *homilia*, being with God.

Our "second founder," Guigo, was well aware of all this. In his personal vocabulary, the immediate encounter with God himself, which is the reason for being of life in solitude, is typically expressed in the notion that "God reveals His secrets to us." (For example, the manifestation of God to Jacob in solitude, cf. *Cons.* 80, no. 4). But at the same time, this meeting makes extensive use of intermediaries and is carried out through a series of concrete activities: the monk in his cell, says Guigo himself (St 4, 2), "will occupy himself in an orderly and fruitful manner, through reading, writing, psalmody, prayer, meditation, contemplation and work." Through all this, our Statutes explain (ibid.), the monk develops the habit of a "quiet listening of the heart."

In this secret life with God, the monk will go through difficult moments, but also moments in which he will perceive his joy. Saint Bruno did not overlook these moments, as presented in this previous citation: "What benefit and divine joy the solitude and silence of the desert bring to those who love them, only those who have experienced them know." And to Rudolf Saint

Bruno says that "the reward for the effort of combat is a peace that the world does not know, and joy in the Holy Spirit" (6).

"For the effort of combat": let us take note of these words. The combat exists, and there is no lack of trying moments. One monk and spiritual master, J. B. Porion, in a letter to a confrere in distress, reveals his secret to us:

> This feeling of weariness, this rapid exhaustion of strength during the day, this lack of savor for everything that is to be done within the framework of Carthusian life — all this is one of the forms of the Carthusian trial, of the agony to which we consented when we hurled ourselves into God as one hurls one self into the sea. The solution would be to endure all of this, day after day, in union with Our Lord; to bear this patient consumption as a dark glory. In one way or another, in the Charterhouse, we suffer this agony: and it is in hoping against all hope that it is given to us to conceive eternal life in ourselves, in the most intimate secret of ourselves. Often a secret to ourselves.

This is another form of *homilia*, of converse with God. In reality it contains a joy, but a secret joy, that of being united with Christ.

Describing Christ's place in our prayer is a delicate matter. The central question is not how much of our thought in prayer should be given to Christ and how much to the Trinity. Explicit thought is not the main question. In fact, the Christ-like character of our prayer is perfectly expressed in the words of Saint Paul: "It is no longer I who live, but Christ who lives in me." It is a question of life.

The heart of Christ's life is the offering of himself, out of Love, to the Father. This is in itself an unfathomable, infinite mystery, and at the same time a mystery that governs the whole history of humanity and of every human being.

We find in ourselves, by grace, an inclination towards the total gift of self to God, to the praise of his glory. This is nothing other than the presence in us of this Mystery of Christ.

This presence in us finds its greatest realization in participation in the Sacrifice of the Mass. Let us think about what M. Olier said about the priest at that moment: "We must annihilate ourselves in this action and be there purely as members of Jesus Christ." Living members, called to live inwardly what Christ lives in this sacrifice.

At the same time, the Mass is the summit of our entire life: all that we may do, and therefore above all every other form of prayer, is in implicit reference to this union in the Mass, and to what Christ lives in it. This is still true when the Mass (or even Christ) is not explicitly present in our thoughts.

But because the Mystery of Christ is so deeply inscribed in our hearts by grace, it is very easy to turn, if the occasion arises, to the recollection of the cross. In no way is this recollection felt as a foreign body in our own meditation!

Ultimately, the "knowledge" of God is an act of love. An episode from the end of the life of little Thérèse says this better than any lecture. Tortured by illness and interior trials, she was no longer able to get out of bed. One day the nurses found her kneeling in bed (how had she managed it?) with her eyes intently fixed on the Crucifix. They asked, "What are you saying to Jesus?" Her answer: "I am not talking to Him. I am loving Him."

Available at
OSVCatholicBookstore.com
or wherever books are sold

In preparation for the Jubilee Year 2025, the Exploring Prayer series delves into the various dimensions of prayer in the Christian life. These brief, accessible books can help you learn to dialogue with God and rediscover the beauty of trusting in the Lord with humility and joy.

Prayer Today: A Challenge to Overcome
Notes on Prayer: Volume 1
by Angelo Comastri
In order to have saints, what is needed are people of authentic prayer, and authentic prayer is that which inflames with a fire of love. Only in this way is it possible to lift the world and bring it near to the heart of God. To pray in truth, we must present ourselves before God with the open wounds of our smallness and our sin. Only in this way will the encounter with God be an encounter of liberation and redemption.

Praying with the Psalms
Notes on Prayer: Volume 2
by Gianfranco Ravasi
This little guide to the Psalms includes four cardinal points: a general reflection on prayer, the breath of the soul; a panoramic look at the psalmic texts; a portrait of the two protagonists, God and the worshipper, but also the intrusion of the presence of evil; and finally, an anthology of brief commentaries on the Psalms most dear to tradition and the liturgy. The hope is that all the faithful may draw fully from this wonderful treasury of prayers.

The Jesus Prayer
Notes on Prayer: Volume 3
by Juan Lopez Vergara
This book explores the unique experience of the fatherhood of God for Jesus Christ, whom he calls Abba — which in his native Aramaic language means "Dad." Throughout his earthly life, Jesus is in contact dialogue with Abba. From his Baptism in the Jordan through his public ministry and ultimately his crucifixion, this relationship will mark him forever, transforming his life, and our lives, too.

Praying with Saints and Sinners
Notes on Prayer: Volume 4
by Paul Brendan Murray
The saints whose writings on prayer and meditation

are explored in this book are among the most celebrated in the great spiritual tradition. The aim of this book is to discover what help the great saints can offer those of us who desire to make progress in the life of prayer, but who find ourselves being constantly deflected from our purpose, our tentative efforts undermined perhaps most of all by human weakness.

Parables on Prayer
Notes on Prayer: Volume 5
by Anthony Pitta

What characterizes, in a singular way, Jesus's teaching on prayer is the recourse to parables. Jesus did not invent a new system for praying. Jesus was not a hermit, a Buddhist monk, or a yogi. He instead chose the daily life of his people to teach prayer with parables. This book explores the parables in the Gospels explicitly related to prayer. The reader is guided by Jesus, the original teacher of prayer with parables.

The Church in Prayer
Notes on Prayer: Volume 6
by Carthusian Monks

Carthusian Monks reside in several international monasteries. Founded in 1084 by Saint Bruno, the Order of Carthusians are dedicated to prayer, in silence, in community. Like other cloistered religious, the Carthusians live a life focused on prayer and contemplation.

The Prayer of Mary and the Saints
Notes on Prayer: Volume 7
by Catherine Aubin
When Mary appears, anywhere in the whole world, the places where she appears have points in common with the biblical places where she stayed and lived. This book reviews these places, examining what they reveal to us about Mary's identity, and what the inner spaces are that Mary asks us to dwell in today. This book also explores the unique relationship two holy women each had with Mary, leading us toward a new, deep revelation of Mary's closeness to each of us.

The Prayer Jesus Taught Us: The "Our Father"
Notes on Prayer: Volume 8
by Hugh Vanni
This book identifies the theological-biblical structure underlying the Lord's Prayer and situates it in the living environment of the early Church. This will give us a framework of reference, and as a result we will see first the antecedents in Mark, then the systematic presentation of Matthew, Paul's push forward, the accentuation of Luke, and, finally, the mature synthesis found in John.